FREE DVD

FREE DVD

Advanced Placement Comparative Government and Politics DVD from Trivium Test Prep!

Dear Customer,

Thank you for purchasing from Trivium Test Prep! We're honored to help you prepare for your AP exam.

To show our appreciation, we're offering a **FREE *AP Exam Essential Test Tips* DVD by Trivium Test Prep**. Our DVD includes 35 test preparation strategies that will make you successful on the AP Exam. All we ask is that you email us your feedback and describe your experience with our product. Amazing, awful, or just so-so: we want to hear what you have to say!

To receive your **FREE *AP Exam Essential Test Tips* DVD**, please email us at 5star@triviumtestprep.com. Include "Free 5 Star" in the subject line and the following information in your email:

1. The title of the product you purchased.

2. Your rating from 1 – 5 (with 5 being the best).

3. Your feedback about the product, including how our materials helped you meet your goals and ways in which we can improve our products.

4. Your full name and shipping address so we can send your FREE *AP Exam Essential Test Tips* DVD.

If you have any questions or concerns please feel free to contact us directly at 5star@triviumtestprep.com. Thank you!

- **Trivium Test Prep Team**

Copyright © 2020 by Accepted Inc.

ALL RIGHTS RESERVED. By purchase of this book, you have been licensed one copy for personal use only. No part of this work may be reproduced, redistributed, or used in any form or by any means without prior written permission of the publisher and copyright owner. Accepted, Inc.; Cirrus Test Prep; Trivium Test Prep; and Ascencia Test Prep are all imprints of Trivium Test Prep, LLC.

The College Board was not involved in the creation or production of this product, is not in any way affiliated with Accepted Inc., and does not sponsor or endorse this product. All test names (and their acronyms) are trademarks of their respective owners. This study guide is for general information only and does not claim endorsement by any third party.

Printed in the United States of America.

Table of Contents

Resources

Practice Examinations

Introduction

The Advanced Placement Comparative Government examination tests your knowledge and understanding of various types of government. Six specific countries are referred to throughout this test. These are Great Britain, China, Mexico, Nigeria, Russia and Iran. The topics included in all AP Comparative Government courses are:

- Introduction to Comparative Politics
- Sovereignty, Authority, and Power
- Political Institutions
- Citizens, Society, and the State
- Political and Economic Change
- Public Policy

Each of these topics will be related to the six countries discussed above, allowing you the opportunity to compare the governmental systems of these six with one another with relative ease. Modern public policy issues, in particular, will offer a helpful tool.

This is a comparative course, so you will learn about governments, including the political and economic impact of government, within each of these countries. You should, after taking the course or preparing for the test, be able to consider the different types of government in relation to one another, their societies and how the government functions, both on a small and a larger scale.

According to the College Board, upon successful completion of the AP Comparative Government course, you should be able to do the following:

- Compare and contrast political concepts, themes, and generalizations across multiple governments and nations.
- Describe and explain typical patterns of political processes and behaviors and their consequences on the people and government.
- Compare and contrast political institutions and processes across countries and to make generalizations regarding political processes and governments.
- Analyze and interpret basic data relevant to comparative government and politics.

You will also be required to understand a variety of different types of tables, graphs and data. If you're quite comfortable with this material, you may not feel a need for review; however, do expect test questions to include representations of various types of social science data on government spending or policies of various sorts.

There is no assigned textbook for the Comparative Government course, and teachers are free to take a variety of different approaches to the course. That said, the College Board does provide teachers with briefs specific to political conditions in several of these countries, which may not be included in your textbook. In this book, you'll find a broad overview of the subject of comparative government. Depending upon your school, you may have taken this course in the fall or spring semester, and might have taken the U.S. Government course before or after it. While not comprehensive, this will provide you with the majority of the information you can expect to see on the AP Comparative Government test, as well as four practice tests. Information included in this guide, including contemporary political discussions dates to 2014. Students should seek out additional information as needed for the exam in future years to maintain a thorough understanding of any contemporary changes in government.

The Advanced Placement Comparative Government test consists of two parts, multiple choice questions and free response questions. There are 55 multiple choice questions, making up 50 percent of your total grade. You'll have 45 minutes in total for this portion of the test. The free response portion of the examination takes up the majority of the test time, 100 minutes. There are eight free response questions in total. Five of these are short answer questions, requiring about a paragraph of response. You'll have three longer essay questions as well. One requires you to answer a conceptual analysis question, while the remaining two questions are country context questions. In the sample essays later in this text, you'll find examples of all three types of questions, along with sample answers in a high, average and low scoring range. For a high-scoring test, you need to do well on both the essay questions and the multiple choice questions. Plan to allow at least 20 to 25 minutes per longer free response question. This allows a total of five to eight minutes per short answer question. Practice will help you to write well under time pressure.

Your personal test preparation strategy may vary depending upon when you took the course. If you took Comparative Government in the fall term and you are preparing for the test in May, you may want to do more review than someone who is just completing the test. You will, of course, also need additional review if you're opting to take the course without having taken the class. For the best results, allow yourself shorter periods of review time frequently over the weeks prior to the test, rather than cramming in the days before the examination.

You can opt to work your way through this guide and your textbook in a straightforward fashion, from beginning to end, or you may begin by taking one of the sample tests in the back of this text. If you opt to take a sample test, grade your test and assess the questions you struggled most with, devoting additional study time to those sections. When you're preparing for the test, take the time to take at least one sample test in circumstances similar to those of the actual test day. Set a timer, work in a quiet room, and limit your access to supplementary materials. It is particularly important that you practice writing under pressure, particularly given the number of questions on the AP Comparative Government exam.

Scoring

The test is scored on a scale of 1 to 5. A score of 5 is extremely well qualified to receive college credit, while a score of one is not qualified to receive college credit. While colleges and universities use scores differently, a score of 4-5 is equivalent to an A or B. A score of 3 is approximately similar to a C, while a score of 1-2 is comparable to a D or F. The examination is scored on a curve, adjusted for difficulty each year. In this way, your test score is equivalent to the same score achieved on a different year. The curve is different each year, depending upon the test. Approximately 46 percent of students receive a 4 or 5 on the AP Psychology examination.

Scores of 4 to 5 are widely accepted by colleges and universities; however, scores of 3 or lower may provide less credit or none at all. More elite schools may require a score of 5 for credit and some schools vary the required score depending upon the department. You will need to review the AP policies at your college or university to better understand scoring requirements and credit offered. While you'll take the AP Comparative Government Examination in May, your scores will arrive in July. You can have your scores sent to the college of your choosing, or, if you're testing after your junior year, simply wait until you're ready to apply to the colleges of your choice.

Scoring on the multiple choice section of the examination is straightforward. You receive one point for each correct answer. There are no penalties for an incorrect answer or a skipped question. You should, if you're unsure, guess. Even the most random guess provides you a one in four chance of a point. If you can narrow down the choices just a bit, your chances increase and, along with them, your possible test score.

The FRQs are scored from 1-8 depending upon the quality of the essay. Essay questions are graded by human graders, typically high school and college psychology instructors. They have been trained to grade the essays by the College Board. You'll find more information on specifics about scoring the free response questions in the chapter that includes the sample essay questions and responses.

Staying Calm, Cool and Collected

Conquering test anxiety can help you to succeed on AP exams. Test anxiety is common and, if it's mild, can help keep you alert and on-task. Unfortunately, if you suffer from serious shakes, it may leave you struggling to focus, cause you to make careless errors, and create potential panic.

- Allow plenty of time for test preparation. Work slowly and methodically. Cramming doesn't help and will leave you depleted and exhausted.

- Remember to stay healthy. Sleep enough, eat right, and get regular exercise in the weeks preceding the AP examination, particularly if you're planning to take several tests during the same testing window.

- Practice breathing exercises to use on test day to help with anxiety. Deep breathing is one of the easiest, fastest and most effective ways to reduce physical symptoms of anxiety.

While these strategies won't eliminate test anxiety, they can help you to reach exam day at your mental best, prepared to succeed.

The night before the test, just put away the books. More preparation isn't going to make a difference. Read something light, watch a favorite show, go for a relaxing walk and go to bed. Get up early enough in the morning to have a healthy breakfast. If you normally drink coffee, don't skip it, but if you don't regularly consume caffeine, avoid it. It'll just make you jittery. Allow ample time to reach the testing location and get your desk set up and ready before the examination starts.

What to Take to the Test

- A sweatshirt or sweater, in case the testing room is cold

- A bottle of water

- Two sharpened No. 2 pencils and two black or blue ink pens

- A wristwatch

And a quick note here: there's no need to take paper along. You'll receive not only the test booklet, but also additional scratch paper to take notes and make outlines for your free response questions. Plan to leave your phone in the car, but you may take a paperback book or magazine into the testing room if you're early.

Tackling the Test

Some people don't find testing terribly anxiety-inducing. If that's you, feel free to skip this section. These tips and techniques are designed specifically for students who do struggle with serious test anxiety and need to get through the test as successfully as possible.

- Control your breathing. Taking short, fast breaths increases physical anxiety. Maintain a normal to slow breathing pattern.

- Remember your test timing strategies. Timing strategies, like those discussed in relation to the free response questions, can help provide you with confidence that you're staying on track.

- Focus on one question at a time. While you may become overwhelmed thinking about the entire test, a single question or a single passage often seems more manageable.

- Get up and take a break. While this should be avoided if at all possible, if you're feeling so anxious that you're concerned you will be sick, are dizzy or are feeling unwell, take a bathroom break or sharpen your pencil. Use this time to practice breathing exercises. Return to the test as soon as you're able.

- Remember that, while this may be an important test, it is just a test. The worst case scenario is that you do not receive college credit and find yourself taking comparative government in college. If you do so, the knowledge you gained in the AP Comparative Government course will help you to succeed.

Comparative Politics and Government

Overview

Comparative politics is both a **method of study** and a **field of study,** by comparison of countries and by examining political phenomena, respectively. This definition can help you frame your studies in comparative politics throughout your test preparation. Remember that comparative politics allows you to look at the similarities and differences in the six countries you have studied. While only six countries are included in the course, the knowledge and skills you've developed in the class can be applied to any country or set of countries, regardless of political system.

A number of key questions will help to guide your study of comparative politics. Read through the following list and take a few minutes to consider how these questions relate to what you know of government, in a broad sense. All of these questions can help you answer a single question.

What is Politics?

- Who has the power to make decisions?
- How did they get power to make decisions?
- What internal challenges do political leaders face?
- What external challenges do political leaders face?

Several different factors, called social cleavages, impact the function of government and politics. These are divisive factors within a society and include race, religion, ethnic differences, economic differences and social classes. These can significantly impact policy-making at all levels.

There are several key terms connected to comparative politics. Many of these are familiar; however, you'll need to understand them properly in context to use them in this course and on the examination:

Key Terms	
State	Political power applied over a set geographic area with clear borders through the various branches of government. The state may be separate from the nation; however, the two terms are often used interchangeably.
Nation	A community of people who identify with a shared culture, values and history.
Government	A collection of people who work together in political institutions or occupy positions of power within the state.
Regime	The rules and institutions that control access to political power. Political regimes may endure beyond a single individual or government and include the various bureaucracies that make up the government.
Institution	The means by which state power is organized. May include branches of government, bureaucracies, and offices, from the most major to the most minor.
Ideology	A way of seeing the world used to make sense of reality and organize information. Political ideology may be influenced by a variety of personal and cultural beliefs.
Civil Society	Non-state organizations people join for their own benefit and betterment, which include a variety of organizations, including labor unions and churches. While political parties are not a form of civil society, civil society may serve a political purpose.
Culture	The experience and characteristics of a group, including their language, art, literature, and belief systems. Multiple cultures may exist within a single state on the basis of religion, ethnicity or class.
Economy	The public or government arrangement to buy and sell goods and services, including personal labor. The economy may exist with limited government controls, as in the free market, or with significant ones, as in a Communist nation.

Government-Sanctioned Institutions	These are created by multiple countries to address shared concerns regarding international well-being, like the United Nations. These institutions are designed to address a variety of global issues, from world peace to health.
Supranational Organizations	Groups of various nations working together toward a common goal. These goals may be economic or not. NAFTA and the EU are examples of supranational organizations.

While governments are defined in part by who holds power and how they use power, they are also characterized by the relationship between the government and the citizens of the country. This relationship includes how people think of the government and interact with the government, how people learn about their government, voting laws, regulations and practices, and any factors within society that might impact participation in government. These factors are similar to the social cleavages discussed earlier and include gender, race, economic class, and ethnicity. For instance, citizens in a democracy vote for their leaders and may engage with those leaders to help create political change. In a more authoritarian government, citizens have no control over their government. Social cleavages can also impact citizen behavior and feeling. You might, as an example, realize that a particular ethnic group is more likely to vote for a certain political party.

While governments may be democratic or authoritarian, they are all, regardless of political system, categorized as unitary, confederate or federal. A unitary government consolidates power in a single location. A confederate system is primarily made up of individual units, like states, with a weak central government. A federal system divides power between local or regional governments and a strong central government. The six countries included in this course are all examples of unitary systems; however, Britain incorporates some aspects of federalism and Nigeria has a relatively weak central government.

Specific theories are often used to discuss politics and, particularly, comparative politics.

1. Political economy emphasizes the connections between politics and economics. It suggests that economics may control policy decisions, even when the decision is not a good one for either the population or the country.

2. Modernization theory is particularly interested in how cultural issues may impact a lack of political development or impede political development.

3. Dependency theory relates social issues, particularly poverty, to the global economy rather than conditions within a single country.

All political systems, regardless of their organization, set policies for the state. These policies are impacted by political ideology and, depending upon the organization of the government, may involve some amount of citizen input.

- Economic performance, both domestically and internationally.

- Social welfare, including health, employment, family-related legislation, education and assistance programs.

- Civil liberties and freedoms. Democratic countries typically protect these freedoms; however, they may be less well-defended or even non-existent in Communist, post-Communist and developing countries.

- Environmental policies protect the environment.

Typically, as you likely learned in grade school, governments can be divided into three branches. The executive branch carries out the laws of the country. In many cases, the executive includes both a head of state and a head of government. In the case of Great Britain, Queen Elizabeth II is the head of state, while the prime minister heads the government. The queen has no political power; however, the opposite is true in Russia, where the head of state holds significant power. The executive branch also includes a variety of other offices or bureaucracies. You may be familiar, in your own life, with some forms of bureaucracy. For many of us in the United States, one that we frequently encounter is our local licensing bureau or department of motor vehicles. These are the primary tool for implementing political policy. German political philosopher defined governmental bureaucracies, identifying a number of traits specific to a bureaucracy.

- Bureaucracies are hierarchical, with a clear chain of command.

- Individuals and offices have specialized tasks.

- The bureaucracy is controlled by a set of rules and has clearly defined goals.

- Bureaucracies promote on the basis of merit. Productivity is more important than personality.

Legislatures make laws and may be bicameral or made up of two houses, or unicameral, with only one legislative house. Membership in the legislature varies, but may be assigned or determined by voters. In a bicameral system, one house may be identified as upper and one as lower; however, this does not typically relate to political power.

The judiciary branch consists of the courts, specifically the constitutional courts. These courts analyze the acceptability of laws within the context of the country's constitution. Of these three branches; the executive, legislative and judicial, the judicial is the weakest.

Several other key factors can impact each of these bodies. Political parties, in a two-party or multiple-party system, can impact the political system within a country in substantial ways. Electoral systems define how votes are cast, who can vote, and how representatives are designated. Regional and electoral boundaries are included as part of electoral systems. Finally, political elites often wield a great deal of power and leadership, regardless of the type of government. Depending upon the government, political elites might be born into a family with political power or progressively work their way up in the political system or within a political party.

Political Change

While there many ways that governments change, we will focus on three here:

- Revolution: This involves a fundamental change to the existing political order in a short window of time.

- Reform: Seeks changes to improve the government without altering its basic makeup.

- Coup d'état: Replaces the leadership of a country, often by violent means. This is often a revolutionary act.

Left and Right

On the next page you'll find a graphic breaking down the traditional definitions of four commonly heard, but often misunderstood, political science terms denoting where beliefs fall on the "left-right" political spectrum.

Left-Wing			Right-Wing
Radical	**Liberal**	**Conservative**	**Reactionary**
• Supports revolution (dramatic political and social change.) • Strongly emphasizes idealism, often with open hostility to existing social and cultural institutions.	• Tends toward fast-paced reform and to view government as representative of social priorities. • Emphasizes use of state power to promote individual liberty at expense of existing order • Opposes majoritarian control of social, political and cultural institutions	• Tends toward gradual reform at a pace that is organic to each unique state. • Emphasizes use of state power to preserve and strengthen social and cultural institutions perceived as beneficial. • Opposes use of state power to influence or change existing social, political and cultural institutions.	• Displays complete opposition to political change in favor of maintaining the status quo. Tends to be nationalist, anti-modern and stringently traditionalist.

Examples of Radicalism	• The American Revolution of 1776
	• The Russian Revolution of 1905

Examples of Liberalism	• Abolitionism and Suffrage Movements
	• The New Deal

Examples of Conservatism	• Constitutional Checks and Balances
	• Privatization and Deregulation

Examples of Reactionary Politics	• The Congress of Vienna, 1815
	• Fascism

Both radical and reactionary beliefs – on the far left and right of the political spectrum, respectively – are often referred to as "extremist," and are more prone to use violent means to achieve their ideological objectives.

Modern Global Trends

In recent years, some overall trends have come to define the international community. There are three trends, in particular, that you should be aware of:

Democratization

Democratization is the most important of these three trends. Democratization requires open, free and competitive elections. There must be a possibility for the current regime to be overthrown in order for a country to qualify as a democracy.

Liberal democracies, including many older democracies, like Great Britain, display a number of other traits that we commonly associate with democracies. These include support for civil liberties, like:

- Freedom of speech
- Belief and assembly
- Due process of law
- A neutral judiciary
- System of checks and balances
- Open civil society
- Freedom of the press
- Civilian control of the military, reducing the likelihood of *junta* or coup d'état.

A country with elections, but lacking these elements, is known as an illiberal democracy. There have been three waves of global democratization, with the most recent beginning 1970 in both authoritarian countries and former colonies. Authoritarian regimes lost legitimacy. Worldwide, the middle class grew in strength and power.

Human rights have become an increasingly important international issue; countries have a tendency to follow their neighbors into democracy, as seen when the Eastern Bloc fell in the 1980s.

The Market Economy

Today, the market economy has become the predominant world economic system; however, there are two types of market economies. A mixed economy incorporates both some central government control and aspects of the free market, while a pure market economy has little or no government control. Marketization refers to the creation of a free market economy, incorporating the trade of goods and labor. Privatization describes the transfer of state-owned enterprise to private ownership.

Ethnic and Cultural Conflict

After World War II, the impact of ethnic and cultural differences on politics was significantly reduced, and many theorists no longer considered it to be a relevant factor in government. That has changed more recently. Nationalism became a more significant factor around the time of the fall of the Eastern Bloc and Soviet Union, which toppled in 1990. While nationalistic forces were more important at that time, in the years since, religion has played a much larger part in political conflict. The stronger role played by religion in many countries has increased, in significant ways, the division between people and countries.

In the Resources section of this book, you will find an entry for Walker Connor's *A Nation is a Nation, Is a State, Is an Ethnic Group, Is a...* from 1978. It's not just us that recommends you read it - it's also highly recommended by the AP College Board!

Comparative Studies

The following chapter provides a brief introduction to essential information about each of six countries we will study in comparison. This particular chapter is primarily geographical, allowing you to gain a better understanding of the country's physical position in the world, as well as any special challenges that country may have experienced that impacted its political development and growth.

Great Britain

Great Britain is an island nation, located to the west of continental Europe, separated by the English Channel. Great Britain is made up of England, Wales, Scotland and Ireland. These individual regions retain some national identity, even today. Britain is relatively small, with limited resources. The climate lends itself to a short growing season, and while the soil is fertile, this short growing window limits food production. Nonetheless, Britain has a relatively dense population, but smaller populations in the northern parts of Great Britain.

China

China is located in Southeast Asia and has the largest population of any country in the world today. In terms of size, China is the third largest country, behind Russia and Canada. Much of China is mountainous, with a landscape made up of mountains, plateaus and foothills. Much of the non-mountainous terrain is made up of large tracts of rich, fertile soil. China is typically divided into four regions: North, South, Northwest and Qinghai-Tibetan. The North and South are home to the majority of China's population. Distinct cultural differences separate these regions.

Russia

The state of Russia extends over much of Northern Eurasia. In total area, it is the world's largest country. Given its large size, it includes a number of different climates and has been shaped by different geographical forces. There are a number of different ethnic groups within Russia, varying in beliefs and cultures. Given the relatively harsh climate, growing seasons are short in Russia, making food supplies a challenge, even today. Many areas of Russia are minimally inhabited, with significantly higher population densities in the cities.

Nigeria

Nigeria is a country a little larger than Texas, located in West Africa. This country has one of the largest populations of any African country. Nigeria's soil is fertile and well-suited to a number of different agricultural crops; however, subsistence farming practices have led to the need for food imports. A large number of different groups coexist in Nigeria, with varying cultural and religious beliefs. Today, the country is approximately 50% Muslim, 40% Christian and 10% Animist. There are significant political conflicts between Muslims and Christians.

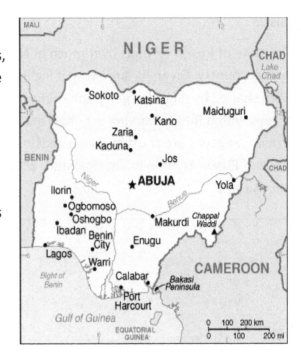

Nigeria has rich natural resources, including oil, and the country plays a significant role in the international commodities market.

Iran

Iran is a Middle-Eastern country, bordered by both the Persian Gulf and Caspian Sea. The population of Iran is approximately 98% Muslim; however, religious and cultural beliefs may differ between groups even within the same faith. While approximately one-third of Iran is arable land, little of this is used and modern irrigation techniques are rarely employed. Food supplies are imported to the country, rather than produced. Iran's primary export is petroleum.

Mexico

Mexico is located in North America, sharing a border with the United States. With a semi-tropical climate and rich fertile soil, agriculture flourishes in Mexico. The country also has a number of natural resources, including gold mines and petroleum. While the Mexican economy has improved in recent years, infrastructure and education remain poor, with a large percentage of the population living in poverty. Mexico includes a number of indigenous ethnic groups, but the majority of citizens identify as Mestizos, recognizing both an indigenous and European heritage.

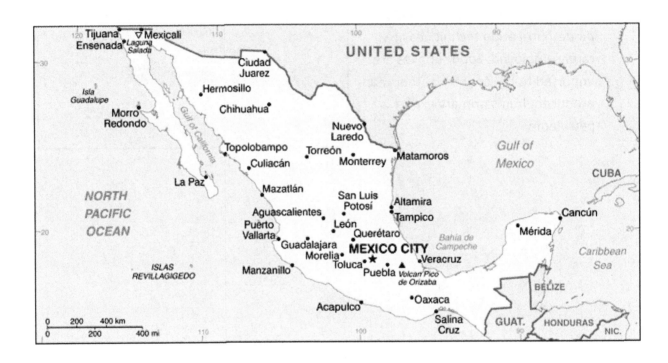

Sovereignty, Authority and Power

Overview

Before we dive into the review content, let's take a moment and define three key terms:

Key Terms	
Sovereignty	The final authority over inhabitants of a given territory
Authority	The right to rule over the people of a region
Power	The ability to make others do what they would not otherwise do

What is a State?

Political philosopher Max Weber, who lived in the early 20th century, defined the state as, "a human community that (successfully) claims the *monopoly of the legitimate use of physical force* within a given territory." [1] In this case, we can understand that the state has control of the army, police and other forces with the power to do violence legally. The state is the entity that is able to allow and authorize the use of force to uphold the law.

In recent years, political theorists have noted that intra-state or internal wars are frequently the result of this loss of authority. Weber's definition of the state has formed the basis for anarchistic movements, but is also a key to understanding how authority and power work within the state.

While Weber's definition of the state has been quite influential, there are several other key factors to consider in this chapter. As noted above, sovereignty is the final authority over the inhabitants of a given territory. This means that the state owes no authority to a higher power. The state can implement policies within its borders without interference or the consent of another body. If the state cannot exercise sovereignty, it lacks autonomy or self-control. Developing countries are more likely to lack autonomy.

Authority is the right to rule. A legitimate government has authority. In a democracy, this authority comes from the people, via legal elections. In an authoritarian regime, it may come through military control.

---

[1] Max Weber, *Politics as a Vocation,* 1919.

Power is the ability to get people to do things that they would not otherwise do. For instance, you might not want to pay taxes. The government has the ability to make you pay taxes by imposing financial or legal penalties on you if you do not. The state also has the power to set laws and to force you to obey those laws, or impose consequences if you do not.

With this broad understanding of political systems and the key terms of sovereignty, authority and power in mind, we will move onto clear discussions of the use of sovereignty, power and authority in each of the six sample countries.

Great Britain

Great Britain is a parliamentary democracy and is the oldest lasting democracy in the world today. Given its age, Great Britain has a well-evolved and stable system of government, including checks and balances to reduce the potential for corruption and implement the use of power successfully. A number of different factors have influenced the British state.

The Constitution and Growth of Parliament

The government of Great Britain is based on a constitution, or a body of fundamental principles or established precedents according to which, a state or other organization is acknowledged to be governed. The British constitution is not a single document, as in the United States. It is a collection of documents, together called the Constitution of the Crown. The two most important documents in British politics are the Magna Carta and the Bill of Rights. The Magna Carta, written in 1215, placed the first limitations on the British crown, including forcing the king to consult the nobility on a number of matters. In 1688, William and Mary signed the Bill of Rights at the end of the Glorious Revolution, granting Parliament a number of additional rights and responsibilities.

It's important to point out here that the Glorious Revolution was not a violent one, but was the result of political upheaval. Also, the British Bill of Rights is not a document guaranteeing individual rights, like the American Bill of Rights.

The Monarchy

While Great Britain is a constitutional monarchy, with a king or queen as head of state, the power of the monarch has been limited for many centuries, with more progressive limitations on that power occurring over time. Today, the monarch of Great Britain serves as a figurehead and symbol of the state, but holds no political power. By the end of the 17th century, Parliament held the most significant political power in Great Britain. The church has been, since the time of the Reformation, of less importance than the government and the monarch is the official head of the Church of England. Religion has remained a source of conflict in Ireland; however, it is a less significant force in the remainder of Great Britain.

The Industrial Revolution: Reform in the State

Britain's democracy has developed largely through a process of reform, rather than revolution. This has not been a violent struggle, but a slow progression over centuries, with only a few sudden upheavals or changes, like the English Civil War and Glorious Revolution. While it was a slow and relatively peaceful progression, it was not without conflict. Some of those conflicts continue to impact Britain today. Two key factors impacted English politics and society, beginning in the 18th century. The first of these was colonialism. During this time, Britain developed a substantial mercantile empire, centered on the nation's colonial possessions. At the same time, the traditional organization of British society dissolved, replaced by a new urbanization. The changing roles in this new society altered who held power and created a new political elite.

Modern Britain

Britain's role within the world and international community has changed substantially since the beginning of the 20th century. Depleted by two world wars, Britain has lost much of its international power. Following World War II, Great Britain established significant social welfare programs, meeting the needs of its people. These were cut back during the 1980s, during a time commonly called Thatcherism, after Prime Minister Margaret Thatcher. Britain continues to struggle with the conflicts between a social welfare state and free market economy today.

China

Empire

Prior to 1908, China was an empire. Until the 19th century, it was a remarkably powerful one, developing a rich culture and strong military. Driven by Confucian values, the state was well-organized, rigid and structured in terms of social classes. During the 19th century, foreign influences, including the opium trade managed by Great Britain, as well as a growing population and inadequate food supplies weakened China. Following the death of Dowager Empress Cixi in 1908, a revolution changed the government of China and the short-lived Chinese Republic came into being.

Revolution

The Chinese Communist Party was founded by Mao Tse Tung (sometimes spelled Zedong) after World War I, as part of the 1920 May 4th movement. The CCP was in conflict with the majority political party, the KMT or Kuomintang, through much of the

1920s; however, the nationalist KMT retained control until 1949. After several years of fighting, the CCP gained control of much of China, pushing the KMT into modern-day Taiwan. The People's Republic of China was established under Mao on October 1, 1949.

The People's Republic dramatically changed the lives of the people of China, working under a number of different five-year plans that included the collectivization of agriculture and industry. China ended diplomatic ties with the west and established a tense alliance with Russia at this time. The redistribution of land led to many challenges, including widespread famines as a result of intentional management of the food supply by the CCP.

Power in the Communist State

To discuss power and authority in China, it is critical to understand that many of the political entities in China hold no actual authority. They serve as figureheads or mouthpieces for the CCP, making decisions based on the will and goals of the CCP, rather than acting independently in any way. In an official sense, there is an executive, legislative and judicial branch; however, all simply do the will of the CCP. There are executive bureaucracies, but all tend to be corrupt, and positions are typically assigned based on the favor of the CCP.

The CCP controls the army, police, and prison system, and has, since early in the history of the People's Republic of China, shown a clear willingness to use force against its own citizens. There is no system in place for judicial review, and prison terms tend to be life sentences.

In more recent years, some economic modernization has occurred as China has found a relatively powerful economic position in the international order. This economic success has provided additional legitimacy to the Communist government in China.

Russia

The Communist government, established during the Russian Revolution, fell in 1990. Under Communism, the state owned all means of production, from food to natural resources to consumer goods. Following the collapse of the Communist state, the means of production were privatized, or transferred from state to private ownership.

The Russian Empire

Prior to the 20th century, Russia was an empire, ruled by a powerful tsar. The tsar, or emperor, sometimes shared power with councils of nobles; however, democratic reforms of the sort seen in the West were quite slow to reach Russia. In the middle of the 19th century, Tsar Alexander II instituted a number of significant reforms, including ending the institution of serfdom, which tied a peasant or worker to the land or an industry, significantly limiting their personal freedoms. Russia remained an absolutist monarchy until the Revolution of 1905, which instituted constitutional reforms and limits on the power of the monarch.

The Bolshevik Revolution

Following significant losses in World War I, the lower classes of Russia began to move forward with revolution. They did not seek the reforms of the Revolution of 1905, but rather a people's revolution, inspired by the work of Marx and Engels. By the end of 1917, the power was no longer in the hands of the tsar and legislature, but now in the hands of the Communist party, or Bolsheviks, led by Vladimir Lenin. The Soviet Union, taking the place of the Russian Empire, and the short-lived Russian Republic, was born in the revolutions of 1917. The transfer of power was not entirely smooth; now, power was concentrated in the hands of the soviets, or worker's groups. Private bank accounts, church property and factories were seized under the new Communist government. The Congress of Soviets elected a Council of People's Commissars to govern the country. The Communist government remained quite authoritarian throughout its reign, from 1917 until 1990. Civil rights were limited and people had little control over their own lives.

The Fall of Communism

During the 1980s, progressive steps toward democratization were taken in the Soviet Union. These were small steps or gradual reforms. Over the course of the 1980s, Communism fell throughout the Eastern Bloc and new, democratic governments gained control of these countries, weakening the power of Communism. By 1989, the people of the Soviet Union were able to vote and had begun to gain some control over their own political fate. The first competitive elections were held in 1990, and with those, the Soviet Union and Communist party fell. Russia remained a large nation, but had a new political future.

Nigeria

Nigeria, formerly a British colony, gained its independence in 1960. The young state was loosely organized, with a weak central government. More than 250 different ethnic groups reside in Nigeria, making the process of creating a central government even more challenging. Fighting between the Christian Ibo peoples and the Muslim Hausa people led to civil war in the late 1960s. The nation remained under military rule until a civilian leader was elected in 1979. At this time, Nigeria was considered an example for other post-colonial countries, with a thriving economy and successful democracy.

Military Rule

In 1984, the military seized control of the government. This was followed by a series of military coups d'état over the coming years. The military government regimes were quite totalitarian, imposing significant restrictions on the people of Nigeria. Ethnic differences, particularly between the Ibo and Hausa, contributed to the challenges. The United Nations reported on a number of human rights violations during this time and the government severely restricted civil rights. During this time, Nigeria played an active role in international affairs within Africa, intervening in a number of disputes in other countries. The corrupt military government and costly wars, as well as poor infrastructure and limited government investment, resulted in significant economic after the country's oil boom in the 1970s; the country's gross national product (GNP) has fallen significantly in the intervening decades.

A Return to Democracy

Free elections in February 1999 resulted in a return to a democratic government. The democratic government of Nigeria includes the president, who is also commander-in-chief of the Nigerian army, a National Assembly and a Constitutional court. These three, including the executive, legislative and judicial branches, are modeled on other successful democracies. While the nation has a democratic government, recent elections have revealed significant corruption in the electoral process. This corruption extends to all facets of the government, and while the government is relatively wealthy, some 75% of Nigerians live in extreme poverty.

Threats to Power

Social cleavages pose the greatest threats to the power and authority of the Nigerian state. In particular, religious issues cause significant tension. A militant Islamic group,

Boko Haram, has recently been responsible for a large number of civilian deaths, kidnappings and other actions. The northern part of Nigeria is dominantly Muslim, and largely under the influence of Sharia, or Islamic religious law. Christians have opposed the spread of Islam, and particularly Sharia. Political insurgents have, on a number of occasions, attacked Nigeria's oil fields, and conflicts over immunization vaccines have led to an outbreak of polio in recent years. Corruption within the government itself has led to splits in the political parties, fostering national instability.

Iran

The 1979 Revolution

Prior to the revolution of 1979, Iran was a relatively liberal, autocratic nation, under the rule of a Persian monarch. While today, Iran is typically characterized in terms of religious fundamentalism, this was not true prior to the 1979 revolution. Before the revolution, Iran was relatively prosperous, and the common causes associated with revolution were not present; however, there was corruption in the government and significant objections to westernization and modernization. This was a religious revolution, and a popular one. Many individuals were exiled following the revolution, including liberals and intellectuals.

The Theocracy of Iran

While Iran, technically, has elections and the right to vote, the nation is a theocracy, and thus an authoritarian government. Power lies in the hands of Islamic clerics and theologians, rather than the people. Individuals running for office must be approved by the Guardian Council. Typically, those that might favor liberal reforms, as well as women, are not approved. Thus, the elections are not, by definition, competitive and the ruling party cannot be ousted. Iran defines itself as an Islamic Republic.

The government of Iran has poor relations internationally and has brought about few positive changes domestically. The government is primarily concerned with the promotion of Islam and limiting secular or Western influences. Educational opportunities and health care for the poor have improved in recent years; however, there are widespread limitations on civil rights in Iran. The Iranian economy has diversified from oil production recently, and was improving prior to the Western imposition of economic sanctions in response to their nuclear energy program. Iran insists that the nuclear program is for peaceful energy production, but countries like Israel and the United States have maintained that Iran is developing the capability to produce nuclear weapons.

Mexico

Power and Authority in Mexico

The Mexican government is, today, relatively well-organized, but not highly centralized. The state is organized according to the terms of Mexico's 1917 constitution. While this constitution has been in place since 1917, Mexico functioned as a one-party system for many of those years. In a one-party system, there is no real choice involved, and thus no democracy.

Mexico's transition to democracy has been relatively slow, but also relatively stable. Mexico's constitution helped to provide stability throughout much of the 20th century, even as other parts of Latin America struggled with government tensions. This one-party rule was an authoritarian government.

Transition to Democracy

Democratization began in Mexico in the 1980s, culminating in the 2000 election of a member of an opposition party to the presidency. Between the middle of the 1980s and 2000, the government invested more money in liberal reform programs and reduced corruption, while opposition parties worked to further their own goals, and eventually found a voice in the government. The transition has been relatively successful; however, Mexico still struggles economically in a number of ways. Since Mexico's states remain largely independent, there is limited control by the central government, so conditions and laws differ. This results in a lack of consistent infrastructure, as well as continued power in the hands of state governments, rather than the national government.

Political Institutions

Overview

Political institutions include the parts of government, like the executive, legislative and judicial branches of government, but also social facets, like political parties.

Democratic Organization

In the first chapter, we discussed the basic organization of the state. In a democratic government, the state includes:

1. A legislative branch, which makes laws

2. An executive branch, which implements the laws

3. A judicial branch, which considers and determines the constitutionality of laws.

All governments, both authoritarian and democratic, rely upon bureaucracies, which are specialized organizations dedicated to a specific function of the state. These bureaucracies, which make up a country's institutions, enable continuity – that is, the state's ability to continue to function despite changes in leadership.

Communist Organization

Communist governments operate in a significantly different manner than democracies. In theory, the founders of Communist ideology, Marx and Engles, essentially believed in a strong, centralized government that enforced the dominant ideology while remaining responsive to a system of representative democracy, with political entities organized by local workers' collectives who used the threat of counter-revolution to keep the state's power in check. In practice, Communist governments throughout history have favored decisions made by the political elite, rather than by the vote of the people.

Totalitarian Organization

In a totalitarian or military regime, the political elite may be legitimate and accepted by the people, or may rule purely through coercive or violent power. Civil rights are typically substantially limited under all types of authoritarian governments.

Great Britain

The parliamentary government of Great Britain includes both a head of state and a head of government, as well as a bicameral legislative branch and independent judicial branch of government. The head of state is officially the monarch; as of 2014, the monarch is Queen Elizabeth II.

The head of state opens Parliament and represents the country's traditions and cultural institutions, but holds only ceremonial political power. The head of government or head of the executive branch of government is the Prime Minister. The remainder of the executive includes a cabinet and a number of ministers. The Prime Minister and all cabinet members are considered parts of the House of Commons.

In England, the legislative branch is made up of the lower house, the House of Commons, and the upper house, called the House of Lords. These are not analogous to America's House of Representatives and Senate, as the House of Lords is not democratically elected, and ostensibly exists to provide expert advice on legislation passed by the House of Commons. However, the House of Lords is made up of political elites, who are often appointed by virtue of family (called peerage, or traditional nobility,) or position within the Church of England. This system grew out of Britain's formerly feudal arrangement, in which commoners and nobles were separated by socioeconomic class.

The House of Commons is elected, rather than appointed, and holds the majority of political power in Great Britain. While some laws are broadly applied, Scotland, Wales and Northern Ireland each have an independent legislature as well.

There are three separate judiciaries in Great Britain, including England and Northern Ireland, Wales, and Scotland. While these act independently, other courts have power over the entirety of Great Britain, including the Supreme Court and other high courts.

Great Britain is commonly deemed a two-and-a-half-party system, with two dominant parties and a third prominent, but less dominant, party. The two dominant parties are the Labour and Conservative parties, with the Liberal Democrats holding a significant minority. The Conservative Party, whose members are commonly called Tories, is a center-right party. As of 2014, it holds the majority in Parliament, working in coalition with the Liberal Democrats. The Labour Party is a center-left party, currently holding a minority interest in Parliament.

China

China is a Communist state, largely governed by the Chinese Communist Party or CCP. China has both a head of state, the President, and a head of government, the leader of the People's Congress. Both positions are figureheads, with the CCP holding actual power in China. The most powerful individual is the Secretary of the CCP. The People's Congress is elected by regional and local People's Congresses; however, the Congress has no true legislative power. In China, the executive and legislative branches of government exist, but serve no significant role in government. There are no checks and balances in place for the actions of the CCP.

China is governed by the CCP and is an authoritarian state, because the true organization of the state – and all political power - lies within the political institution of the party. There are, technically, multiple political parties in China, but apart from the CCP, they are mere tokens.

The CCP is organized according to principles set forth in the Marxist tradition by Vladimir Lenin during the Russian Revolution of 1905. The CPC's National Congress convenes every five years. During the intervening years, the Central Committee meets annually. Day-to-day work responsibilities are under the control of the Politburo and the Standing Committee. These organizational bodies are not technically part of the executive, legislative or judicial branches of the Chinese government, but they are the ruling power, with control over making and enforcing laws, the army, and national finances.

Russia

Today, Russia is a post-Communist state that identifies itself as a democracy. The state is organized into executive, legislative and judicial branches and the people do have the right to vote in relatively free elections, though that has been compromised in recent cycles.

Russian Democracy

Following the end of the Soviet Union, the newly-created Russian government passed a constitution in 1993. The structure of the government includes a president, who holds significant power, a prime minister, with less power, a bicameral legislature made up of the Federal Council and the State Duma, and a judicial system administered by the Ministry of Justice. The president is elected by popular vote and is also commander-in-chief of the Russian army. The prime minister is appointed by the president, and the Federal Council or upper house of the legislature is made up of representatives of member nations of the Russian Federation. The members of the State Duma are elected from party-lists through proportional representation. The people vote for a party, rather than an individual, and then a number of seats is assigned to the party based on the number of votes received. The judiciary includes three levels of courts, with the highest, the Constitutional Courts, deciding on matters of law.

An Illiberal Government

While Russia meets the essential criteria for a democracy, by holding free, relatively uninhibited elections and allowing the populace a necessary voice in the government, it is an illiberal rather than a liberal government. The government has little interest in the civil rights of the Russian people, and has reduced access to civil society, limited the rights of the people to organize. The government imprisons those who protest its policies, works to stymie the political power of the press, recently passed laws limiting the rights of gay and lesbian citizens, and has made moves in recent months to interfere with Russian citizens' free, open access to the Internet. Human rights violations are common in Russia. Notably, the government is legitimate, and retains the support of the people, even in the face of civil rights violations.

Russia as a Military State

The president of Russia, as commander-in-chief of the army, is capable of using the army to meet his goals and the goals of his political power. While international military efforts are commonly under the control of the United Nations and other alliances, Russia has, as of May 2014, engaged in a complicated campaign of military action and espionage against a neighboring country, Ukraine.

This, combined with its illiberal treatment of its own citizens, has led many experts to believe that Russia's young, post-Communist democracy is on the road to collapse.

Nigeria

The Nigerian democracy is quite young, and is impacted by a number of social challenges; however, to understand them properly, you must understand the country's basic institutions.

The Nigerian Government

The Nigerian government is a federal republic, based largely upon the organization of the United States, as well as that of Great Britain. The executive branch is led by the president, who heads a number of ministries and serves as both head of state and head of government. The president appoints ministers, but they must be confirmed by the Senate. The nation has a bicameral legislature, consisting of a House of Representatives and Senate. These two chambers make up the totality of the legislative branch, or the National Assembly. Theirs is a multi-party system, with approximately six parties represented in the legislature. While there is universal suffrage, accusations of corruption in the Nigerian elections are common.

The judicial branch is somewhat more unusual as four distinctly different types of law co-exist in Nigeria. The Supreme Court heads the judicial branch of the government, and, as in the United States, serves as a constitutional court. The four types of law that co-exist in Nigeria include English law, derived from Nigeria's past as a British colony, common law, or law developed since independence, customary law which comes from indigenous customs and practices, and Sharia or Islamic law, in use in the northern parts of Nigeria.

Iran

Iran is a theocracy, or a nation ruled by religion, in this case, the values, thoughts and ideology of Islam. The Islamic Republic of Iran dates to 1979, as does Islam's constitution. Shi'a Islam is the state religion of Iran.

Iranian Political Organization

The state of Iran has an elected president and parliament, or Majlis. There is also an elected Assembly of Experts. The power of both the president and legislature is limited by the role of religion in the government. The Assembly of Leaders selects the Supreme Leader of Iran and may remove him from office if it is deemed necessary. The Supreme Leader appoints judiciary officials, controls the military and appoints some members of the Guardian Council, and, given his role in selecting the judiciary, has substantial control of the Guardian Council.

Religion and the State

While there are elections, all those running for office must be fully investigated and approved by the Guardian Council. The Guardian Council, made up of appointed theologians selected by the Supreme Leader and individuals chosen by the judiciary, has significant power within Iran. The Guardian Council has the right to approve all members of parliament, as well as the president, and has veto power over all laws passed within Iran. The Guardian Council is a religious body, designed to ensure that the state is acting in full accordance with Islamic Shi'a law.

Mexico

The United Mexican States is a young democracy, with a federal government. While the constitution is not new, the transition from an autocracy to a democracy is.

The Republic of the United Mexican States

The Mexican government is divided into three parts: the executive, legislative and judicial. The executive branch includes the president, elected by popular vote. The legislature is bicameral, made up of the Senate and the Chamber of Deputies. The judicial includes a number of different courts, with the highest being the Supreme Court.

The states within the country of Mexico are relatively autonomous and self-governing. The governor of the state holds executive power within the state. The states may not make treaties with one another or foreign powers, but may otherwise act largely independently of the federal government. Each state has its own constitution. When compared to other nations, you can see that the federal government of Mexico is significantly weaker, with less power, than that of many other, more centralized nations. Mexico City is not located within any state and serves as a political, cultural and economic capital.

As discussed in the prior chapter, for many years, the government structure was in place, but it was an autocratic, one-party system. Today, a number of different political parties operate in Mexico. There are three significant parties: the PAN, PRI, and PRD. The PAN is a right of center party, while the PRD is left of center. The PRI is the majority party. Smaller parties operate on a local level or by forming coalitions with the larger three parties.

Citizens, Society and the State

Overview

There can be no state, no nation and no government without the people. Understanding how the people interact with, participate in, and even feel about their government will help you to recognize the differences between governments. This chapter will also include a discussion of how the state treats its own people, with regard to civil rights and services. You may find it helpful to think about the citizen and the state as a relationship between two parties, both with rights and responsibilities. While we have thoroughly defined and discussed the state, as an entity, the following terms will help to facilitate your understanding of this chapter.

Key Terms	
Citizen	A legally recognized subject or national of a state
Society	A large group of people connected through interactions
Norms	Unspoken rules or conventions within a society
Race	A large group of people that share specific physical traits
Ethnicity	A large group of people that share a culture, history and a belief that they share common descent. Ethnicity is not defined by physical traits.
Religion	The organized system of belief in a superhuman, divine power, often with accompanying morals and values. In the case of social cleavages, religion and ethnicity have frequent areas of overlap.
Gender	The perceived differences in behavior, traits and roles between males and females
Class	Social class divisions and differences are a form of social cleavage related to economics. The notions of class have fueled revolutions, including the Industrial Revolution and the revolutions in Russia and China.
Social Movement	Informally organized groups working together for a common cause

You should recognize that much of the material in this chapter concerns norms and behavior, rather than structured political groups or institutions.

Political Participation and Social Cleavages

Social cleavages are the ways in which we identify ourselves. These may include national identity, gender, race or ethnicity, religion, social class, or other factors. Linguistic, religious and cultural differences can intensify these cleavages. When a national identity does not mesh with state boundaries, cleavages are more likely to occur.

- Cross-cutting cleavages occur when an individual's various identities allow them to identify with a variety of different groups. Someone raised in the rural south who is working at a high-paying job in Washington D.C. may feel both a connection to the poor southerners of his childhood and his colleagues and peers at work.

- Complementary cleavages occur when different identities and factors result in similar attitudes. This may lead to an intensification or more extreme behavior. A good example is the increasing polarization of American politics between conservatives and liberals. These may also be called coinciding or polarizing cleavages.

Identity

Social cleavages are based on your personal identity. You have multiple identities or cleavages, some that you are consciously aware of, and some that you may not recognize. These cleavages are the result of your gender, race, ethnicity, religion, education, upbringing, and income. You may find it helpful to take a few moments to think about the words you would use to describe yourself. Some social cleavages are even self-selected. You might, for instance, identify with a particular social movement or even identify yourself by a hobby or personal passion. Each of these can be a form of social cleavage.

Social Movements and Interest Groups

Social movements are informal, loosely organized groups working toward a common political, social or economic cause. These are not interest groups, which are both more specific and organized. Social movements include environmentalism, women's rights, or worker's rights. Individuals involved in these movements may well also belong to various interest groups.

Understanding social movements is essential to fully understanding how citizens function as a part of society and how political change occurs. According to political scientist Charles Tilly, there are several distinct categories of individuals who participate in social movements. Modern scholars arrange these into slightly different, but somewhat comparable categories. These include:

1. Zealots participate in social movements with little regard for their individual preferences. These are today's core activists in a social movement.

2. Run-of-the-mill participants are sympathetic to the cause, but not as strongly committed. Today, these are considered the participants in a movement.

3. Misers support the goals, but only participate if they see value to themselves. These may be called contributors today.

4. Opportunists participate only for the value to themselves. This group most closely parallels the sympathizers in modern terminology.

Interest groups are more specific and significantly more organized than social movements. While environmentalism is a social movement, Greenpeace is an example of an interest group. Interest groups act as a link between the general population and those who are part of the social movement and the government. They advocate for their goals and desires, both economically and politically.

Economic groups are typically related to business interests, while advocacy groups are related to a particular cause. Interest groups are most successful when they are large and well-funded. When an interest group has deep pockets and significant financial backing, it can typically achieve significantly more political change. The relationship of the state and interest groups varies depending upon the country. In many countries, interest groups work to influence politicians, while in others they may play a more active role in the state.

- In a pluralist system, groups are autonomous, and multiple groups may coexist.

- In corporatism, the state sanctions some peak organizations. These organizations may act as umbrella organizations for smaller organizations committed to the same cause.

- When state corporatism exists, the state is responsible for the creation of interest groups. The groups have minimal autonomy.

- In a state-controlled system, groups are created and managed by the state, and have no autonomy.

Political Participation

Political participation includes all activities designed to influence the leaders and political decision-making in the state. In most cases, the general populace in both democratic and autocratic states knows less than the political elite and is less likely to participate in the political process. Conventional political participation includes voting, writing to your representative, joining a political party and donating to political causes.

In an autocratic state, political participation is typically limited to the political elite. Political activity, even conventional activity, may be seen as a threat to the authority of the state. Unconventional participation includes political activity not sanctioned by the government. Boycotts, strikes, and terrorism are all characteristic of unconventional participation. Finally, non-participation is a factor in every type of government, even democracies. In democracies, the young, the underprivileged, and minorities are less likely to participate in government.

Mass Media

The mass media, including television, newspapers, radio and some internet sites, is a key means of encouraging political participation and informing citizens about the state. In an autocratic state, the mass media is typically state-owned. Democratic states may own media corporations, but work to insure the freedom of the press within the state.

Civil Society

The term civil society is quite broad, encompassing all sorts of civic, professional and religious organizations. You likely participate in a number of these organizations as part of your own life. For American high school students, groups like the National Honor Society are an example of civil society. Civil society plays a different role in each type of government. In an autocratic government, many types of civil society may exist; however, they are not allowed to become political. Civil society is stronger in a democratic government.

Great Britain

Great Britain is a largely homogenous culture, almost universally English-speaking. Ethnic minorities make up a very small amount of the total population. National identities, social class differences, and religious tensions are the most significant social cleavages in Great Britain.

There are four distinct national identities in Great Britain: English, Welsh, Scottish and Irish. Politically, the English are dominant, and have been so throughout history. Wales has maintained some aspects of its national culture, even after being under English rule since the 16th century; however, Wales is economically depressed compared to England. The Scottish people, united with the English in the early 17th century, retain a strong national identity as Scots, rather than British. Northern Ireland has been the source of greatest conflict, with the remainder of Ireland freeing itself entirely from British rule. Religious tensions remain in Northern Ireland even today.

Social class divisions have been an issue throughout British history. The clearest of these is the distinction between the upper and working classes in Britain. This division is often less financial and more related to personal identification. Someone raised in the working class is likely to continue to identify as working class, even if they have reached a higher income level. The education system, in which the upper class attends "public" boarding schools, has supported this division.

As of 2001, approximately seven percent of the British population was not of European descent. Ethnic minorities in Britain are primarily from former colonies. Tensions between minorities and British communities have occurred occasionally; however, this is a relatively minor social cleavage in British society.

Political participation is relatively high in Britain, with approximately 70 percent of eligible voters voting with some regularity. Party allegiances fall roughly along class lines, with members of the working class typically voting for the Labour party and members of the upper classes more likely to vote for the Tories.

While there are a variety of social movements in Britain, prominent interest groups include trade unions, as well as more conservative corporate interests. The British government owns and controls the British Broadcasting Corporation or BBC; however, there are a number of competitive television and radio stations. The government does not allow political advertising on the BBC or commercial networks.

China

Interactions between the Chinese state and the citizens of China are impacted by both Communist party politics and Chinese tradition. While the Communist party is the most significant political force in the country, only around eight percent of the population has joined the CCP. In the past, China has responded to political social movements with violence, as occurred in Tiananmen Square in 1989, when the military killed hundreds of pro-democracy protestors, including children who were present at demonstrations, and injured thousands more.

The only interest groups or social movements with any level of political pull in China are those approved of and officially tolerated by the Communist party, like the national trade union for factory workers. In urban areas, workers' groups, called danwei, are a common means of both organizing and controlling workers. These groups not only control access to pay, but also medical care, childcare and other needs.

Russia

The citizens of the Russian Federation have witnessed a significant transition during recent decades. They have left a Communist government behind and moved through a transitional government, progressively reaching toward democracy. While the Communist state nominally advocated equality among all people, there are a number of social cleavages present in today's Russia.

Nationality makes up the most substantial social cleavage within the Russian Federation. Approximately 82 percent of the population is Russian, but there are sizable minorities of Tatars, Ukrainians, Chuvashes, Bashkis, Byelorussians, and Modavians. These populations within the federation maintain some degree of autonomy and most find it relatively beneficial; however, the Chechnyan people and Chechnya have engaged in violent acts, strongly seeking independence in recent years.

Religious and social class differences are minimal in many areas of Russia. There is some anti-Semitism present, as well as anti-Muslim sentiment, particularly given the rebellion in Muslim-dominated Chechnya. Most Russians identify as non-religious. The Communist government, in control for much of the 20th century, was largely successful in reducing social class differences among Russians. There are significant differences in the beliefs and education of urban versus rural populations.

Under the autocratic Communist system, individuals were required to vote in party elections, but the choices were largely non-existent. While early participation in free elections was relatively low, voter participation is progressively increasing in modern Russia.

During the Communist regime, there was limited access to interest groups; however, a wealthy class developed following the end of Communism. These wealthy corporate owners, including family members of former Russian president Boris Yeltsin, can be identified as an interest group in modern-day Russia.

Nigeria

Religion and ethnicity are the two most significant social cleavages in Nigeria. These are frequently complementary, leading to the creation of extremist groups and movements. The Hausa-Fulani in North Nigeria have both a cultural and religious cleavage. Past civil wars have been the result of these differences. Linguistic cleavages further separate the citizens of Nigeria. While the official language of the state is English, different ethnic groups speak their own languages. These are not typically cross-cutting cleavages and it is difficult for the Nigerian government to establish common ground and work toward unity.

Civil society in Nigeria is commonly divided along ethnic and religious lines; however, there are several significant business organizations. Student organizations have been responsible for some amount of political uprising and women have also attempted to organize, although not yet entirely successfully. While many people work in agriculture, there is no organization in place for farmers to support their efforts.

Political participation varies in Nigeria. The people can participate conventionally, in elections and working for elections. While conventional participation is an option in Nigeria, the strong cleavages and identities within the country have led to significant violence. As of 2014, many observers believe that Nigeria may be on the brink of war or genocide, as groups from the Muslim north attack villages, kidnap and murder. Nigeria does allow for freedom of the press, with most people gaining their news and information from the radio.

Iran

As a theocracy, Iran attempts to create an image of unity; however, social cleavages exist within the Islamic state. These include class, ethnicity and even religion. Frequently, these cleavages overlap with one another.

In broad terms, the lower classes, including individuals in rural and urban areas, are more religious, embracing fundamentalism. The state shares these religious views and has provided some improvements and enhancements to gain the loyalty of the lower classes. Since the revolution, the middle class has become significantly smaller, but has remained largely secular. Resistance to the Iranian government is most likely to come from this class of people. They are culturally liberal, and stubbornly so, even as their economic well-being has fallen since the revolution. Following the revolution, the majority of the upper class left Iran. There are a number of ethnic minorities in Iran, each with a distinct culture and language; however, ethnicity is a relatively unimportant political factor.

Social movements in Iran are primarily religious in nature. The impact of religious interest groups has led to significant social change since the revolution; however, social movements have also preserved some elements of traditional Persian culture. Students and women have attempted to organize and invoke change, but have had relatively limited success in the face of the strongly theocratic government. There are no significant interest groups, and people participate in the political process through limited Iranian elections, rallies and petitions.

While civil society was limited to religious groups immediately after the revolution, a strong, educated culture sympathetic to the West remains. The Iranian press and cultural media act within a range of limits imposed by the state, particularly with regard to criticism of the government or religion.

Mexico

Social cleavages, civil society, social movements and interest groups all impact the relationship between the Mexican people and the state. As noted in our past discussions of Mexico, conditions in the state have changed significantly in a relatively short time.

Region, ethnicity and class have all impacted the people of Mexico. Religion is not a social cleavage in Mexico, as the vast majority of the population is Roman Catholic. There are a large number of ethnic groups in Mexico, including many groups with indigenous roots. A relatively large percentage of the Mexican population identifies as one of the indigenous tribes, rather than as a mestizo, or person of mixed European and indigenous heritage. Class divisions in Mexico are quite extreme, contributing to cleavages between rich and poor. Finally, regional differences contribute to cleavages, particularly since different regions may maintain quite different policies and may have resentment toward more developed regions, including the capitol city.

Prior to changes in the government of Mexico that embraced democracy, civil society was quite minimal. Mexico was a corporatist state, with the government specifically favoring some interest groups. In democratic nations, corporatism sometimes favors the working class, but in an authoritarian and autocratic state, that is not the case.

Corporatism broke down during the democratization process and today, civil society in Mexico is more pluralistic.

The Mexican press is now quite free and helps to support the burgeoning democracy, by reporting honestly on government issues, including political scandals. This is relatively new, as throughout much of the 20th century, the press was relatively censored, reducing access to information.

Mexico has relatively high voter turnout rates. As citizens of the young democracy, many voters are excited to have a true voice in the running of the nation.

Political and Economic Change

Overview

Profound and significant change is the clearest trait of modern politics. Each of the countries included in this course has experienced a substantial political change, or multiple substantial political and economic changes, during the 20th and 21st centuries. In nearly every case, political and economic changes are intrinsically linked, often in multiple ways. Change can take a number of forms, including creation, consolidation and collapse.

Earlier in this text, we identified the three basic forms of change: reform, revolution and the coup d'état. We also specified several sets of beliefs that impacted change. All of these will be discussed in significantly more detail in this chapter, with specific notes and references as to how change occurred in each of the sample countries.

Revolution and Coups D'état

Revolution

A revolution is a fundamental change in political and social systems. Revolution is typically driven by the people and when this is the case, can be considered a grass-roots (bottom-up, rather than top-down,) effort. Revolutions can vary, but may alter all forms of society. For instance, in Great Britain, the industrial revolution changed the laws, gave additional power to the working classes, saw the movement of the population from the countryside to the cities and fundamentally changed agriculture and the lifestyle of the people. Keep in mind that revolutions can be violent, or can be peaceful and largely concerned with social norms. For instance, the Russian Revolution of 1917 was quite violent, but the Glorious Revolution in Great Britain was largely bloodless.

Coup D'état

While a coup d'état may result in many of the same consequences as a revolution, the coup d'état does not have broad public support. A coup is more often controlled by a small group, often a military group, rather than by a larger part of the populace, particularly the working classes. A coup d'état may or may not be violent and can lead to a regime change, or may retain traditional aspects of the state and bureaucracy. A coup d'état is more likely when the existing government is not legitimate. A coup may or may not lead to a revolution.

Civil wars, as opposed to wars with other countries, are another form of change in government. Civil war is often quite low-tech, and almost always violent. Guerilla warfare is common in rural areas and may include individuals who are not part of an organized militia.

Liberalization

Political liberalization is typically reform, rather than revolution. Liberalization can take a number of different forms, but is typically progressive. It may happen relatively rapidly, with a regime change, or somewhat more slowly. Liberalization is not equated with democratization. Liberalization may include increasing freedoms and civil rights within an autocratic government.

Democratization is the transformation from an autocratic government to a democratic one. The process may vary, but the non-democratic government must fall, remove itself, or collapse to make room for democracy. The transition may be relatively quick, thorough and complete, may stall at a transitional stage between autocracy and democracy, or may be a slow and ongoing process. The process has several stages.

1. Breakdown of authoritarianism. This can occur as a part of government liberalization, coming from above, or can come from a popular grassroots movement.

2. Establishment of democracy. This includes drafting a constitution, either through an assembly or a referendum.

3. Consolidation of democracy. This establishes a stable system of government, unlikely to return to an authoritarian system. There are a number of traits consistent with a consolidated democracy. These include free and fair transitions, peaceful transitions of power, surviving threats, legitimacy and adherence to the rule of law.

Democracies can also collapse in a progressive series of failures, eventually leading to an authoritarian system or to re-equilibration, when the democracy survives. The two steps to failure are crisis and breakdown.

Economic liberalization removes price restrictions, privatizes industry and encourages investment. It may occur as part of political liberalization or separate from it. New economic policies can come into existence without changes in civil rights; however, changing economic policies may lead to political liberalization or even democratization.

Economic change can come in various forms. Today, liberalization is the most common form as countries push toward a market economy.

- Nationalization occurs when the state takes ownership of means of production. While this is often connected with Communism or authoritarian governments, some democratic states retain a number of rights, including mineral and oil rights, as nationalized industries.

- Privatization is the process of selling off government owned commodities to private citizens. This occurred when the Soviet Union fell and has also happened in Russia.

Economic development is progressive, moving from more restrictive economic systems to more open, less controlled systems. While these broad traits help to define economic development, you may also consider economic development in terms of the goods produced. In a more developed society, those goods are likely to involve more advanced technology. In a less developed society, goods are typically more basic, designed to meet essential needs. New products and new technologies help to encourage economic development.

- Economic growth is an increase in a state's economic production over time. The measurement of economic development is the gross domestic product or GDP.

- Gross national product or GNP is used less often today, but refers to the total value of all goods produced by the citizens of the country.

- Purchasing power parity, or PPP, takes cost of living into account. To opt for an easy-to-understand comparison, think of the cost of living in a rural area in America versus a major city; the PPP of the same income is higher in Des Moines, Iowa than New York City.

Nations use a wide variety of different economic strategies. The goal of all of these is to increase the overall economic production within the country; however, their success varies.

1. Import substitution industrialization, or ISI, encourages the development of industry within the country, relying upon various industrial incentives.

2. Structural adjustment focuses on progressive integration into the global marketplace, relying upon privatization.

Levels of economic development are defined in quite specific terms. An economically developed country, or an EDC, has a high GDP and large middle class. Less developed countries, or LDC, have a low per capita GDP, a small middle class and are likely to be less educated and experience higher infant mortality. Newly industrialized countries are those that are rapidly increasing in terms of GDP and quality of life. Countries in transition have some traits of an LDC, including lower per capita GDP, but have the education levels and services of an EDC.

Critical Theories of Economic Development

Two theories are critical to understanding economic development.

Modernization

This is the belief that the current economic systems of Western Europe and the United States are ideal, and that other countries should be proceeding toward a similar "modern" economy. Alongside modernization theory, some dependency theorists believe that modernized EDCs should employ strategies to reduce the economic development of LDCs.

Globalization

Globalization is the process of increasing interdependence between nations, including both EDCs and LDCs. Interconnectedness is facilitated by modern technology, trade and transportation. While dependency theory suggests that EDCs hope to keep LDCs from developing, globalization encourages democratization and development in LDCs.

Great Britain

Great Britain is an economically developed country. It has a large middle class, significant per capita GDP and supports a variety of industries. The most important recent developments and changes in Britain began during the Industrial Revolution.

Between 1832 and 1884, voting laws changed to include not only the wealthy, but first the middle classes and eventually the working classes. Women achieved suffrage in 1918, after World War I. These progressive reforms contented the working classes and prevented the development of strong Marxist movements among them, like those found in Russia that helped to bring about the Russian Revolution. Labor unions, a form of interest group, date to the same period. Labor unions and other workers' rights organizations encouraged pensions for seniors, education for children, limited work hours, and provided for safety in the workplace.

The nation joined together after World War II to implement a variety of new social welfare programs to help the working classes. These included nationalized health care, improved access to education, better care for the elderly and welfare payments for the poor. The reforms following WWII remained largely in favor until the government became more conservative in the late 1970s and 1980s, under Prime Minister Margaret Thatcher. Some of the reforms under Thatcher have been repealed recently, with greater public support for social welfare programs.

China

Modernization in the Chinese Communist state began in 1978, under CCP leader Hua Guofeng. He implemented several specific changes in the state economy, enabling China to join a global marketplace. These include an open door trade policy, with both Communist nations and capitalist western nations, like those in Western Europe and the United States. He instituted broad educational reforms that encouraged, for the first time since the revolution, higher education and scientific research. Finally, he institutionalized the government, reorganizing the state along pre-revolutionary lines, including a less centralized government. Given the sweeping changes it is currently undergoing, it is reasonable, for comparative purposes, to separate the post-revolutionary Chinese economy into two eras: the early years (1940s – 1980s) and the present (1980s onward), as the two are quite different.

Agriculture, industry and all means of production were collectivized following the Maoist revolution. This process occurred in several distinct phases. During the first, peasants were organized into larger farm collectives, made up of around 250 households. During the Great Leap Forward of 1958-1966 under Mao, these collectives were increased in size to several thousand families each. Similar collectivization occurred in industry. These collective farms were a significant failure, and living standards remained very poor throughout much of the 1970s. The collectives were dismantled in the 1980s, placing more responsibility on the individual. Private businesses were allowed after 1988, contributing to the significant growth of industry and international trade in China. Township and village enterprise, or TVE, is the fastest-growing part of the economy, providing significant growth in rural communities.

Russia

Under the Communist regime, Russia suffered economically. Living conditions were poor and the country had a low per capita GDP. Economic factors were a key contributor to the reforms of Perestroika and eventually, the fall of Communism. In the Communist Soviet Union, all means of production were owned by the state, including agriculture and industry. Wages and benefits were set by the state, limiting class differences. While this reduced class differences, it meant there was little hope for significant improvement, and quality of life suffered significantly.

In the 1980s, Mikhail Gorbachev introduced a series of economic reforms. These were market economy reforms, but were never fully implemented. Gorbachev hoped to retain many aspects of the centralized government, while still integrating elements of a more liberal economy. The reform attempts led to conflict within the Politburo, or ruling body, and the eventual collapse of the Soviet government.

Under Boris Yeltsin, conditions worsened for the Russian economy. During the chaos that followed in 1991, a small group of investors favored by Yeltsin gained control of a significant portion of the economy. The economy completely collapsed in 1997, creating significantly worse conditions for the people of Russia. Many were unemployed and Russian currency was devalued. The economy improved slightly in the late 1990s as privatization began to work. From 2000 to 2007, the Russian economy experienced significant growth, including foreign investment. Quality of life and per capita GDP improved dramatically during this time.

Iran

Before the revolution, Iran was a relatively prosperous state, with a large middle class. Universities were open to both men and women, and Iranian culture and tradition supported learning and education. Oil and manufacturing provided for a stable economy, prior to the oil crisis of the 1970s. Following the revolution, the new regime, made up largely of religious clerics, was economically incompetent. Clerics in Islam had, traditionally, avoided any interest in the economy, so the new theocracy was not prepared to manage the economic needs of the state.

The Iranian economy, formerly relatively stable, weakened dramatically in the early 1980s. A number of factors contributed to the failure of the Iranian economy.

1. The Iranian government, like many authoritarian regimes, nationalized many industries.

2. Skilled professionals and the educated classes left the country after the revolution.

3. Following the revolution, western countries, including Europe and the United States, were unwilling to invest in Iran.

4. Oil prices fell internationally.

5. The Iran-Iraq War was costly, lasting more than eight years.

Within the government, there were a number of conflicts and disputes among theologians and clerics with widely different perspectives:

- Pragmatists encouraged a free market economy, contact with the West, and were concerned with the economic health of Iran.

- Radicals favored nationalization and supported the lower classes. Their approach included the redistribution of wealth; this was common among younger and more militant clerics.

- Conservatives objected to the ideas of the radicals, fearing conflict with Western powers and desiring to play a significant role in the international community.

Today, Iran continues to struggle economically. Both inflation and unemployment are quite high. Oil remains the most significant export in Iran today. Iran has increased foreign trade and placed individuals with business and economic experience into positions of power. The state retains control of the Iranian economy, even as foreign trade increases. Education has improved; however, professional identity and economic well-being remain low.

Nigeria

In modern Nigeria, there is a huge gulf between the rich and the poor. While the country was economically successful in the 1970s, today, there are relatively few people living in opulent comfort while the masses are impoverished.

At the time of independence, Nigeria had rich oil reserves, produced adequate food for its own people, and had a number of different agricultural exports, including cocoa beans. Higher oil prices in the 1970s increased oil revenues for Nigeria. During the 1970s, Nigeria invested substantially in manufacturing or industry, but allowed agriculture to fall into decline. The government paid little attention to issues of infrastructure for the people, so modern transportation, health care and communication was largely ignored.

The price of oil dropped substantially in the 1980s, causing an economic crisis in Nigeria. In 1985, as Nigeria was about to default on a number of loans from the World Bank, the Nigerian government instituted a number of economic reforms, called austerity measures. These were unacceptably harsh for the people and were suspended relatively quickly.

Today, approximately 60 percent of the Nigerian population lives below the poverty line and the per capita GDP is only US$900 per year. The government continues to work to improve the economy; however, even with oil revenues, political instability continues to threaten Nigeria's economy.

Mexico

Through much of the 20th century, the Mexican state retained control of the government, favoring policies of import substitution industrialization, or ISI. This promoted local business and industry, offering government support to locally-owned manufacturers. The state also nationalized a number of industries, including Mexico's oil reserves. This was a successful strategy, and Mexico prospered economically from the late 1930s through the 1970s.

The collapse of oil prices in 1982 triggered an economic depression in Mexico. This led to significant economic change, including the process of neoliberalization. Neoliberalization favors a true free market economy over a system like ISI, with extensive privatization of industry and minimal government involvement in the market. Under the new regime, the government also eliminated all welfare benefits, including housing and food allowances, for the poor. Many industries closed down and unemployment rose dramatically. These economic changes culminated in the North American Free Trade Agreement or NAFTA. This agreement helped to increase exports from Mexico, but did not provide for any sort of economic integration between Mexico, the United States and Canada. NAFTA did tie Mexico's economic success to the success of the United States, so as the U.S. has experienced a recession, so too has Mexico.

Public Policy

Overview

Public policies alter some aspect of social, political or economic conditions. There are many different types of public policy, including foreign policy, domestic policy, economic policy, and social welfare policies. Public policies are a useful tool to compare governments, particularly since policy has a particularly significant impact on the lives of the citizens. Public policy is, critically, created by government and applied to the citizens. The governments creating public policy may be national or regional.

Policymaking varies depending upon the country and type of government. In a democracy, laws specifically define how policy is made by lawmakers. In some democracies, both the judicial and executive branches may also play a role in policymaking. In authoritarian governments, policymaking is often more arbitrary. Policies may be made by a ruler or small ruling council and are likely to be influenced by as small group of people and designed to benefit that group, rather than the population as a whole.

Domestic Policy

Domestic policy affects the citizens of a country and seeks to improve social, political or economic conditions in the country. These policies may be designed to meet the goals of the larger population or of only the political elite, and include a broad variety of policy, from education to economic incentives.

Policy is foreign or domestic based upon its target, not its cause. For instance, economic struggles might lead to changes in both; however, increased or decreased tariffs would be a matter of foreign policy, while hiring incentives would be a matter of domestic policy.

Economic Policy

Economic policy focuses on both revenue or income and expenditures or spending. These policies may include debt reduction, budgeting, taxation, setting interest rates, and economic foreign policy decisions.

Fiscal Policy

Fiscal policy describes both expenditures and taxation. Taxation is, for many countries, a significant source of income and revenue. Many nations require an annual budget, accounting for government revenue and spending. A deficit occurs when spending exceeds income. Nations account for this deficit by borrowing, either from an international bank, another nation, or through selling bonds.

Monetary Policy

Monetary policy concerns the money or currency used in the country. This includes the amount of available currency, as well as the interest rate on loans issued by banks. The independence of banks varies from nation to nation. In some countries, the banks are state-owned and operated, while in others, they are largely independent of state control.

Developmental Policy

Developmental policies exist to improve economic development. In a developing country, these are of critical importance; however, they may also exist in economically developed countries, particularly during times of economic recession or depression. Developmental policies vary, but can include market controls, economic incentives, and tax cuts. The World Bank and International Monetary Fund provide aid to developing countries; however, that aid is typically contingent upon free market economic policies.

Trade Policy

Trade policy concerns exports moving out of a country and imports moving into a country. Typically, trade policy refers to goods, either raw materials or produced goods. Free trade agreements encourage imports and exports between different countries. NAFTA, discussed in the previous chapter, is an example of a free trade agreement.

Tariffs and Quotas

Tariffs and quotas are used to reduce imports. Tariffs are charged on imported goods, but may not be charged on all goods or goods imported from all countries. Quotas limit the amount of goods that may be imported to a given country.

Immigration and Citizenship Policy

Sometimes called identity-related policy, these policies define who is a citizen, who may enter the country, how to become a citizen or legal resident, and the rights and responsibilities of citizenship. These policies also address issues of racism, ethnic minorities and diversity within the country.

Citizenship Policy

Citizenship policies define citizenship by birth, as well as the conditions for naturalization. They include policies regarding dual citizenship.

Immigration Policy

Immigration is the process of moving to a country with the intention of living there for some time. Countries have specific policies regarding immigration, including rules about employment, sponsorship, and health.

Integration Policy

Integration policies are designed to support diversity and reduce discrimination against different ethnic groups. These may include hiring and educational requirements, measures to preserve cultures, or other policies specific to the needs of the country and its residents.

Social Welfare Policy

Social welfare policies typically have the most significant impact on the daily lives of the citizens of a country. Social welfare includes a broad range of services and benefits, from education to health care. While the term may, for American students, bring to mind services for the poor, social welfare programs apply to all citizens. Some countries, like Great Britain, are identified as welfare states. These countries provide their citizens with a broad range of services, including health care and old-age pensions.

Eldercare Policy

Eldercare or old age policies provide care for the elderly. The most common forms of old age care are pensions, or monthly checks to support basic needs. Typically, the government funds these pensions through contributions from current, younger workers. While these pension programs are popular with the people and essential for the well-being of the elderly, shrinking birth rates in recent years and an aging population have caused financial challenges for old age pensions.

Health Care Policy

Health care is a public policy issue, particularly with an aging population. Government spending on health care is increasing internationally each year, both in response to age-related health and modern health crises. Just as older people typically require more care and more costly care than the young, poorer individuals also require more health care than wealthier ones. Rural areas, often home to larger populations of the poor, frequently have limited access to hospitals or even basic medical care.

Antipoverty Policy

Policies intended to assist the poor vary from country to country. These have had variable success depending upon the nation. Anti-poverty policies include the redistribution of wealth, as witnessed under Communism, as well as monthly payments or other forms of aid, like housing or food assistance. Programs designed to improve access to education or employment may also be included in antipoverty policies.

Educational Policy

Education is an essential part of social welfare policy. A well-managed and designed educational system reduces poverty throughout the country over time. Depending upon the country, the educational system may be centralized and managed by the national government or it may be regional, with significant variations from one area to another. Access to education may vary, but the typical goal is to allow everyone in the population access to education. Higher education makes up the final piece of educational policy – it includes funding for education, as well as access to universities.

Regulatory Policy

Regulatory policies include a wide variety of laws and rules. These include civil and criminal law codes, policies to regulate businesses, and policies concerning energy and the environment. Laws and rules specific to groups of people, including laws that limit rights and civil rights legislation, are both forms of regulatory policy. Regulatory policy is the broadest category and an important one, impacting a wide range of parts of life.

Foreign Policy

Foreign policy may be defined as the rules, regulations and policies that dictate how countries interact with one another. These are not trade policies, although those also relate to international relations. There are several significant elements to any nation's foreign policy.

National Security

National security policies are designed to keep the residents of a country safe from outside threat. In some cases, national security policies may also address criminal activity, including terrorism or drug trafficking.

National Defense

Policies surrounding national defense regulate all military forces within the country, as well as any military activity outside the country. National defense policy also controls treaty negotiations with other countries regarding weapons.

War

Armed conflict and participation in armed conflicts is the final stage of foreign policy. Nations define, using foreign policy, when and how they will go to war.

Supranational Organizations

Foreign policy also includes participation in supranational organizations, particularly the United Nations. When countries choose to join the United Nations or U.N., they accept and agree to a number of specific foreign policy regulations. They also agree to participate in military peacekeeping efforts managed by the United Nations.

How Policies Are Made

Policymaking can occur in a variety of ways. The legislature may make laws that are applied as policy, through the legislative procedures present in a particular country. In some cases, the executive may produce policy, either through declaration or through the actions of various government bureaucracies. Bureaucracies are, in fact, the source of most government policymaking. There are typically levels within the bureaucracy, with upper-level members able to make rules and regulations that are applied as policy.

Public policy allows the government to function and fosters stability within the state. Stability provides the government with legitimacy and reduces the risk of regime change, whether through legal elections or revolution.

Great Britain

Public policy in Britain deals with the economy, foreign relations and social welfare. Several issues, in particular, have posed a challenge in Britain in recent years. These include:

1. The interactions between the government and the economy

2. Relationships with the EU

3. The balance between alliances with the United States and alliances with the EU

4. Devolution

British foreign policy is primarily concerned with relationships between Great Britain and its allies, including the other countries in the European Union and the United States. Historically, Britain remained largely separate from the rest of Europe, engaging in wars rather later than other nations or avoiding them entirely. Britain finally decided to enter the Common Market in 1960, but was initially refused access to the Common Market, not joining until 1978. The Common Market was the precursor to the European Union.

Britain is one of the signers of the Maastricht Treaty, creating the European Union, but has not chosen to adopt the currency of the EU, the Euro. Labour party politicians favor close relationships with the EU, while more conservative Tories express reluctance about these relationships.

Britain and the United States have had a close relationship since World War II. With growing alliances with continental Europe, that relationship has posed some policy challenges. When the United States began the war in Iraq, it did so with the support of British Prime Minister Tony Blair. This caused divisions in the Labour Party, as well as opposition from the British population. Both France and Germany disapproved of the war, causing additional tensions.

Devolution is a process of dissolving portions of the government and creating new, national governments with some powers for Scotland, Wales and Northern Ireland. While the majority of power remains in England, these national assemblies have growing power. The assemblies may act independently; however, they are dependent upon Parliament. Their existence may be repealed. Additional national power was well-received by the citizens of these countries and helped to reduce social cleavages caused by national identity.

Interactions between the government and the economy are a critical policy issue in modern Britain. These public policy issues include social welfare policy and economic policy. Britain is a welfare state, with substantial social welfare programs for its people, most established after World War II. These include state-run single payer healthcare, the National Health Service. Under Margaret Thatcher in the 1980s, access to some forms of social welfare were cut. Modern Britain has been in an economic recession for some time and under the Labour party some of those social welfare programs have been reinstated. Some of these are accepted by the general public, including the National Health Service, while others are less well-liked.

China

Public policy in China is significantly more complex than in other nations. While the basic goals of economic success and well-being are shared in non-Communist countries, in China, there is a clear conflict between participation in a free market economy to insure economic success and the values of the CCP. This becomes clear in a cycle called fang-shou.

Fang-shou refers to a cycle of economic reform, followed by democratization, followed by a tightening up of policy by the CCP. This cycle has recurred repeatedly. Economic changes lead to increased prosperity. The people begin to demand new rights and freedoms. In responses, policy is changed, either to further limit rights, or to punish those asking for them, often violently. In 1989, students protested in Tianamen Square in Beijing. Their protest was peaceful, but the CCP sent the Chinese army into Beijing and declared martial law. It is unclear how many protesters died, but estimates suggest it was several hundred (while some Western estimates place it at several thousands.) Today, the United Nations and international watchdog organizations continue to question China's human rights abuses.

China's economic policy reforms have been remarkably successful; it is poised to become Asia's largest economy in the near future. Entrepreneurs are free to start businesses and most industry is privatized. Agriculture is no longer collectivized. With these changes, income inequality and class differences have increased significantly. Under more conservative leadership, some of the changes made in the late 1990s and early 2000s have been revoked since 2005.

One of the most significant policy challenges for modern-day China has to do with population. Faced with a large population, China regulated child-bearing in 1979, allowing most couples to have only a single child. While there are a number of exceptions to this policy allowing couples to have two children, it has resulted in a significant population decline. Unfortunately, this leaves China lacking the employee resources needed to support an aging population. Furthermore, Chinese culture favors male children over female ones, and there is now a significant gender disparity, with far more men than women in the young population. This may be the result of infanticide, sex-selective abortion or abandonment. There is an ethnic disparity in this law, with non-Han Chinese allowed more children than Han Chinese. Rural families and those with a disabled or female first child may also be allowed a second child.

As a Communist nation, China maintains a number of social welfare programs, including universal health care and unemployment insurance. In 2013, a new, relatively high, minimum wage was set. Additional social welfare support is available for smaller ethnic minorities.

Russia

Public policy in Russia has changed significantly from the revolution through the collapse of the Soviet Union to today. Internationally, Russia, as a part of the Soviet Union, was a superpower through much of the 20th century. That is not true today. Today, Russia forms a relatively weak part of the international community. The 15 former republics of the Soviet Union have formed the CIS or Confederation of Independent States. This relatively loose organization has not been without conflict and is much less powerful than comparable organizations, like the EU. Growing Russian militarism and nationalism led to the 2008 invasion of Georgia and growing tensions with the Ukraine in 2014.

Domestic policy has, relatively recently, favored strengthening the central government, limiting civil rights in favor of a stronger and more cohesive Duma or assembly. This is typically well-accepted by the Russian people. Social welfare policies are limited. The population of Russia is decreasing, relatively significantly, as a result of both lower birth rates and poor overall health.

Iran

Public policy in Iran is particularly challenging. Technocrats favor closer economic ties with the West, but do not favor any particularly liberal social reforms. Clerics typically prefer more insular policies, isolating Iran from Western influences. This has led to a number of international challenges, including trade and economic sanctions.

After the revolution, Iran favored comprehensive social welfare policies, embracing improvements in education and working on recreating the damaged health care system. While post-revolutionary Iran strongly supported separate gender roles and restrictions on women's dress and behavior, education was open to women. Several public health crises are a factor in Iran today, including drug use and HIV. Recent policies encouraging smaller family size have been successful in reducing the population growth rate.

Nigeria

Nigeria's government faces a number of serious challenges. The young democracy is quite unstable and is currently threatened by social cleavages, violence and concerns about genocide.

Economic policies must address the widespread poverty in Nigeria, as well as the nation's debt. While the IMF favors austerity measures, these must be balanced to avoid causing famine and further poverty in the country.

In order to stabilize the government, Nigeria requires full civilian control of the military, an end to ethnic and religious disputes, and respectful and well implemented public policy to address poverty, health care, education and the HIV crisis in Nigeria.

Mexico

Changing policies under the young Mexican democracy have improved conditions both internationally and domestically. New bureaucracies were created to address human rights issues, and those have reduced human rights violations. Corruption has lessened, but not disappeared.

Social welfare programs, including anti-poverty policies, encourage education, offer small business loans and provide other incentives. These new neoliberal policies have replaced older ones, and are focused on helping the poorest of Mexico's people. NAFTA created a number of jobs in foreign-owned factories; however, many of these hired predominantly female workers, causing an increase in male unemployment. Many young men leave Mexico to work in the United States, either legally or illegally. They are often an essential source of income for families in Mexico. While Mexico has attempted to improve conditions for immigrants living illegally in the U.S., this effort has been unsuccessful.

Resources

Vocabulary

1. Agents of Political Socialization
2. Anarchism
3. Authoritarian Regime
4. Autocrat
5. Bicameral/unicameral legislatures
6. Branches of government
7. Bureaucracy
8. Causation/Correlation
9. Charismatic
10. Checks and balances
11. Civil society
12. Common Law
13. Communism
14. Competitive Elections
15. Confederate government systems
16. Conservatism
17. Corporatism
18. Democratization and types of democracy
19. Demographics (ethnicity, class, etc.)
20. Development—import substitution
21. Devolution vs. Integration
22. Electoral processes
23. Federal government systems
24. Globalization
25. Head of government vs. head of state
26. Illiberal democracy
27. Interest Groups
28. Judicial review
29. Legitimacy and authority
30. Liberalism
31. Linkage institutions
32. Market Economies
33. Marketization
34. Neo-Liberalism
35. Parliamentary Regime
36. Party systems (one, two, multi)

37. Patron-client networks
38. Plurality (First past the post, winner-take-all) elections
39. Political Culture
40. Political socialization
41. Politics of protest
42. Presidential vs. Parliamentary regimes
43. Proportional representation
44. Referendum
45. Regime change vs. Government change
46. Revolution
47. Semi-presidential
48. Separation of Powers
49. Social cleavages (cross-cutting v complementary)
50. Socialism
51. Sovereignty
52. Supranational organizations
53. Technocrat
54. Totalitarianism

References

Images

All maps are in the public domain and were retrieved from the Central Intelligence Agency's World Factbook.

Practice Examinations

Sample Short Answer and Essay Responses

You will find five short answer questions on the AP Comparative Government examination. The test allows 30 minutes total for these five questions, so you should spend approximately six minutes writing about one paragraph for each short answer.

In this section, you will find a single sample short answer question, along with three sample answers: one high-scoring, one average, and one low-scoring.

Sample Short Answer Question

How does Sharia law differ from secular law?

High Scoring Response

Law codes vary from nation to nation and in some countries, may include multiple codes of law. For instance, in Nigeria, there are both secular courts and Sharia courts. While secular law is defined by the state, Sharia law is traditional Islamic law, as defined by clerics. Sharia law applies to matters of family and religion, but is would not be used, for instance, to define a business tax code. In Iran, all matters covered in Sharia law are tried and decided in a Sharia court. While Sharia law is in use, in many cases, a secular court will try cases involving non-Islamic individuals. If you are not Muslim, you are not held to the rules and laws of the Sharia court.

Average Scoring Response

Sharia law is Islamic law, applied in Islamic countries. Both Iran and Nigeria use Sharia law. Sharia law is decided by clerics and religious authorities, rather than the state courts or lawmakers. Sharia courts handle private matters, rather than civil law. Secular courts handle all types of law, not just religious cases. Sharia courts are not found in most non-Islamic countries. Courts in these countries are secular, rather than religious.

Low Scoring Response

Sharia law is religious law, used in Muslim countries. Secular law is decided by the courts in all other countries. Sharia law may not deal with every issue, so even Islamic countries may have some secular laws not handled by the religious courts.

Essay Overview

You will answer three essay questions on the AP Comparative Government examination. One will be conceptual, focused on a broad concept in comparative government. The other two questions deal with a specific country, rather than multiple countries. The questions will tell you to identify, explain or discuss. In this sample section, you will find examples of both types of questions, along with three sample answers for each questions. These answers, like the short answer responses earlier in this chapter, are ranked according to quality. You will find high, average and low scoring responses for each of the two sample questions in this section.

Sample Essay Topic #1

Identify the nation with the longest history of democracy and explain how the nation transitioned from a monarchy to a democracy.

High Scoring Essay Response

In many of the countries we have studied, democracy has been relatively young. That is not true of Great Britain. Great Britain is the oldest, stable democracy in the world. While violent revolutions sometimes lead to democracy, Britain moved from an authoritarian monarchy to a democracy with a series of slow, gradual reforms. The documents that make up these reforms are, together, called the Constitution of the Crown.

In the Middle Ages, the first limits were placed on the monarchy through a document called the Magna Carta. The Magna Carta created the English parliament, in its first incarnation. While the rights of Parliament were relatively limited at this stage, this was, fundamentally, the beginning of a constitutional government. In the 17th century, following the English Civil War and the Restoration of the monarchy, King William signed the Bill of Rights. This Bill of Rights increased the rights and responsibilities of the English parliament.

While these steps were critical in creating the beginnings of a democratic government, there was still a significant need for reform. During the Industrial Revolution, the growing middle and working classes began to demand legal change. Reorganizations distributed seats differently and the vote was progressively extended to larger portions of the population. By the end of the 19th century, Britain had achieved universal male suffrage, although women would not get the vote until after World War I.

As voting rights increased, so too did the powers of the House of Commons over the House of Lords. While the House of Lords was originally dominant over the House of Commons, today, the House of Commons is the more significant legislative power. Alongside this change, the power of the monarch was reduced, leading to the monarch's role as head of state, while the prime minister is the head of government. The progressive changes and reforms allowed Great Britain to transition relatively peacefully from an absolutist monarchy to a parliamentary, democratic government.

Average Scoring Essay Response

Great Britain has a long lived democracy, achieved through slow reform rather than war and revolution. In the medieval period, Britain was a monarchy, ruled by a king. This continued through the Renaissance, with the monarch having absolute power. The monarch acted as he or she chose, with no checks and balances on his behavior.

Parliament was created in the Middle Ages, as the House of Lords. The parliament originally had relatively little power, but was expected to approve new taxes. Parliament was created by the Constitution of the Crown. The creation of parliament shared some amount of power with the nobility, but not necessarily with the common people.

During the Glorious Revolution, the powers of Parliament increased significantly and in doing so, the rights of the king were now limited. Over time, these rights were further limited and the rights of the parliament increased. The king now had to have permission from parliament for a number of state decisions, including taxation and war.

By the industrial revolution, the rights of the people, including the lower classes, increased. Seats in the House of Commons were redistributed, allowing more representation from the growing cities and laws were changed to allow some in the working classes to vote.

Progressively, the elected Prime Minister gained power and the monarch lost power until, today, the monarch is simply a figurehead with executive power resting in the office of the prime minister and the lawmaking abilities of parliament.

Low Scoring Essay

Britain has a democratic government, with a parliament and prime minister. The British parliament has been around for a long time and was created by the Constitution of the Crown in the 17th century. The British democracy was created in a number of different steps, moving gradually toward democracy.

The Magna Carta was the first part of the British democracy. Not much changed for a long time, until the Glorious Revolution. The Glorious Revolution wasn't a war, but did increase the power of parliament. After that, there was a balance between parliament and the monarchy.

The monarch remained really powerful through the 19th century, but the people gained more power over time. The House of Commons became more powerful and people got the right to vote. While all men could vote, women were not allowed to vote until the 20th century.

Today, the monarch is the Head of State, but parliament makes the laws and the executive branch is led by the prime minister.

Sample Essay Topic #2

Discuss the ways in which collectivization impacted Communist countries and the people of those countries, offering at least two specific examples.

High Scoring Essay

Collectivization, or the transfer of ownership of land and means of production to the state, was an essential part of both the Russian Revolution and the Chinese Revolution. In The Communist Manifesto, Marx and Engels envisioned a world in which the state provided for the people, while the people worked for the state. It was a symbiotic and healthy relationship. It did not, however, take this form in reality.

Stalin instituted collectivization relatively early in his reign, once the nation had stabilized somewhat. In the newly collectivized Soviet Union, the majority of food production took place on very large pieces of land, owned by the state and farmed by the peasants. The kulag class or wealthy peasants was destroyed by force by Stalin and his forces. The collective farms looked nothing at all like Marx's ideal, particularly in areas that had resisted the collectivization. Faced with poor harvests, Stalin increased quotas on the farmers in the Ukraine. These higher quotas took all of the grain available, leaving nothing to feed the people, including the farmers and no seed grain for the following year. Widespread famine followed, but this was not a natural famine. Stalin engineered the famine that destroyed the people of the Ukraine, formerly the richest agricultural land in the Soviet Union. Millions died in this famine, called the Holodomor. Approximately 7.5 million people died in the Ukraine in 1932 and 1933.

Collectivization produced a similar result in China. The famine in China began in 1959, only a year after the Great Leap Forward set the collectivization process in motion on a grand scale. Many people were diverted from farming and forced to work in the steel industry. The provinces reported high grain harvests and procurement totals were set quite high. As in Russia, these quotas left no food for the peasants. There was, however, grain in warehouses and the country exported grain. While the exact numbers are unknown, as many as 36 to 45 million people died in this famine. Today, the Chinese government claims the famine was the result of natural conditions and innocent mismanagement, not intentional starvation.

Collectivization was less an accidental failure and much more a tool of the political elite. The intentional starvation of the peasant class reduced the population, limited any potential uprising and helped to secure the power of the Communist state. Starvation was a tool of control, and one wielded by both of these nations.

Average Scoring Essay

Collectivization turned individual or relatively small farms into massive collective farms owned by the state. These massive farms were only a single part of the tragedy of collectivization. While large-scale farms were not an efficient choice, they were far worse than merely large farms. These massive farms were used to control the peasants, decimate the population and gain control.

In Russia, Stalin used collectivization to manage the Ukraine. The farmers of the Ukraine resisted collectivization, but it was forced. These massive farms were expected to produce food for the people of Russia's industries and cities. Quotas were set for the peasants on the farm, and they were only allowed to take their rations after those had been made. The very high quotas were set to create famine in the Ukraine. This famine completed weakened the Ukraine, eliminating any resistance and killing millions.

A similar plan was used in China. Collective farms were given overly large quotas and harsh punishments for any theft of food. Millions starved in the Chinese countryside while food went to waste in the cities. This was both intentional and fully understood. The party used it to weaken the masses and force obedience.

Collectivization led to inadequate food supplies. Adequate food required household responsibility, eliminating the large-scale collective farm.

Low Scoring Essay

Collectivization is a part of the Communist idea, as the farms are owned by the state and worked by the people. The state owns the land and all of the food produced by the land. Since the state owns all of the food, it has to provide rations to the people. It isn't a very good way to run a farm and results in reduced food production.

The low food production led to famine and the people starved in both Russia and China. This was made worse by poor harvests. In China, this happened after the Great Leap Forward. In Russia, it was in the 1930s, after the Revolution. Many people, particularly peasants in the countryside, died from starvation. In both countries, the government tried to cover up the famine and keep it from public knowledge.

While large collective farms remained in the Soviet Union, quotas were made lower after the famine and farms were managed better. In China, collective farms were replaced by household responsibility, providing an incentive to work harder and produce more food.

Practice Test I

Multiple-Choice

1. **GDP stands for:**
   a. Gross domestic product
   b. Great domestic party
   c. Grand democratic product
   d. Great domestic product

2. **The PRI is:**
   a. A British political party
   b. A branch of the CCP
   c. A Mexican political party
   d. The ruling party of Nigeria

3. **The Labour party is:**
   a. Favored by the middle class
   b. Affiliated with the working classes
   c. Quite centrist
   d. Relatively right-wing

4. **The first elected leader in Russia was:**
   a. Mikhail Gorbachev
   b. Vladimir Lenin
   c. Boris Yeltsin
   d. Vladimir Putin

5. **Mao Zedong was:**
   a. The last Chinese emperor
   b. The founder of the Chinese Communist party
   c. The leader of the Chinese revolution
   d. Killed in the revolution

6. **Which is the most significant social cleavage in Mexico?**
   a. Religion
   b. Nationality
   c. Ethnicity
   d. Class

7. **Which is the least significant social cleavage in Russia?**
    a. Nationality
    b. Religion
    c. Ethnicity
    d. Class

8. **The Hausa people of Nigeria are predominantly:**
    a. Christian
    b. Animist
    c. Muslim
    d. Non-Religious

9. **How did geography impact the political development of Great Britain?**
    a. It supported a strong monarchy
    b. It allowed democracy to develop
    c. It prevented war
    d. It encouraged self-reliance

10. **Given the climate and geography in Russia, you can expect a relatively high likelihood of what kind of shortage?**
    a. Lumber
    b. Food
    c. Coal
    d. Metals

11. **Autonomy is:**
    a. A totalitarian government
    b. A democratic government
    c. Civil rights
    d. Self-direction

12. **Bureaucracies are typically part of:**
    a. The legislative branch
    b. The military
    c. The executive branch
    d. The judicial branch

13. The first document limiting monarchial power in Great Britain was:

    a. The Constitution of the Crown

    b. The Magna Carta

    c. The Declaration of Independence

    d. The Bill of Rights

14. Which British monarch signed the Bill of Rights?

    a. Henry VIII

    b. Charles I

    c. William

    d. James I

15. A coup d'état describes:

    a. A democratic government

    b. Revolution

    c. A military takeover

    d. Sudden, unauthorized regime change

16. Max Weber was:

    a. A British politician

    b. A German philosopher

    c. A Russian revolutionary

    d. A British rebel

17. Sovereignty refers to:

    a. Authority within the state

    b. International authority

    c. Nations working together

    d. An autonomous military

18. China is a:

    a. Communist state

    b. Post-Communist state

    c. Confederate system

    d. Military dictatorship

19. An illiberal democracy is one lacking:

    a. Universal suffrage

    b. Women's rights

    c. Competitive elections

    d. Civil rights

20. Privatization refers to:
   a. Government ownership
   b. Private ownership
   c. The sale of government-owned properties to private owners
   d. The sale of private properties to the government

21. Which of the following is least likely to support a free press?
   a. Liberal democracy
   b. Illiberal democracy
   c. Totalitarian government
   d. Military government

22. Recent changes in Russia have led to:
   a. Increased civil rights
   b. Increased reforms
   c. Increased conservatism
   d. Increasing reactionary behavior

23. While China is a Communist country, it is experiencing:
   a. Modernization
   b. Privatization
   c. Revolution
   d. Democratization

24. Perestroika refers to:
   a. Democratization in the Soviet Union
   b. Reform in the Soviet Union
   c. The Communist revolution
   d. The dissolution of the Soviet Union

25. Devolution is currently occurring in:
   a. Russia
   b. China
   c. Great Britain
   d. Nigeria

26. The Maastricht Treaty:
   a. Ended World War I
   b. Dissolved the Soviet Union
   c. Provided for trade with the United States
   d. Created the European Union

27. The most significant source of income in Nigeria is:
    a. Manufacturing
    b. Oil
    c. Coal
    d. Agriculture

28. The IMF is:
    a. A branch of the United Nations
    b. A peacekeeping force
    c. A world bank
    d. A political party

29. A bicameral legislature has:
    a. One house
    b. Two houses
    c. Multiple houses
    d. Close ties to the executive

30. The government of which country is closely modeled on the United States and Great Britain?
    a. Nigeria
    b. Mexico
    c. Russia
    d. Iran

31. Which of these countries is currently the least politically stable?
    a. Iran
    b. Nigeria
    c. Russia
    d. China

32. Sharia law is used in which of these countries?
    a. Iran, Russia
    b. Nigeria, Iran
    c. Russia, Britain
    d. Mexico, Nigeria

33. The Guardian Council is primarily composed of:
   a. Lawyers
   b. Politicians
   c. Clerics
   d. Workers

34. Women lost the most status following revolution in which of the following countries:
   a. Russia
   b. Mexico
   c. Iran
   d. Nigeria

35. Which of these countries qualifies as a welfare state?
   a. China
   b. Mexico
   c. Iran
   d. Great Britain

36. Which country in the Russian federation has sought independence the longest?
   a. The Ukraine
   b. Chechnya
   c. Russia
   d. Siberia

37. Boris Yeltsin's government created:
   a. A monarchy
   b. An oligarchy
   c. A theocracy
   d. A democracy

38. The collectivization of agriculture in Russia following the revolution led to:
   a. Improved production
   b. Famine
   c. Reduced work ethic
   d. Lower production

39. Tiananmen Square refers to:

    a. The site of the revolution

    b. The site of Mao's death

    c. A massacre of Chinese protesters

    d. A memorial in China

40. Prison without trial is an example of:

    a. A human rights violation

    b. Revolutionary action

    c. A civil rights violation

    d. A public policy violation

41. In which of these countries is someone most likely to be imprisoned without a fair trial?

    a. Iran

    b. Great Britain

    c. Mexico

    d. China

42. The Central Committee of the Communist Party in China meets:

    a. Monthly

    b. Yearly

    c. Weekly

    d. Every five years

43. Antipoverty programs are part of:

    a. Health care policy

    b. Education policy

    c. Social welfare policy

    d. Identity-related policy

44. The poorest country included in this course is:

    a. Nigeria

    b. Russia

    c. Iran

    d. China

45. A reactionary is likely to:
   a. Seek out progressive reform
   b. Encourage violent revolution
   c. Look to turn back reforms
   d. Believe current conditions are ideal

46. "Five-Year Plans" are associated with:
   a. A coup d'état
   b. Democracy
   c. Authoritarianism
   d. Communism

47. The developed world's most significant demographic problem is:
   a. Aging
   b. Overpopulation
   c. Infant mortality
   d. Child mortality

48. Which British public policy has caused the greatest conflict within the EU?
   a. Social welfare
   b. Trade
   c. Education
   d. Defense

49. A theocracy is a government led by:
   a. Military authority
   b. A charismatic leader
   c. Clerics and theologians
   d. An elected leader

50. The expanding role of the United Nations is an example of:
   a. Modernization
   b. Democratization
   c. Globalization
   d. Privatization

51. Which of the following is a requirement for a functional democracy?
   a. Multiple political parties
   b. Legitimate, competitive elections
   c. International acceptance
   d. Voter acceptance

52. **Which is a difference between interests groups and political parties?**
    a. Fundraising
    b. Political offices
    c. Special interests
    d. Changing legislation

53. **The party system in Great Britain is best defined as a:**
    a. Single party system
    b. Two plus party system
    c. Two party system
    d. Multi-party system

54. **The most significant law-making body in Great Britain is:**
    a. The House of Lords
    b. The House of Commons
    c. The Prime Minister and cabinet
    d. The Queen

55. **The Politburo in Russia is comparable to:**
    a. The Supreme Court
    b. Parliament
    c. Cabinet
    d. Committee

Short Answer Questions

1. How did the collectivization of agriculture impact rural China?

2. Which of these countries chooses to embrace past culture, even though there are substantial differences between that culture and the modern nation? Identify the country and briefly explain.

3. What is Glasnost?

4. Define globalization and give at least one example of how it has impacted the countries studied.

5. How has privatization impacted Communist and post-Communist countries? Identify at least one example.

Essay Questions

1. Explain the international response to recent events within Russia, including the Chechen rebellion and the annexation of the Ukraine.
2. Identify three ways in which the history of Iran or Islam is important for modern day Iran and how these have shaped the state.
3. Compare and contrast at least two examples of democratic reform with two examples of revolution, democratic or not.

Multiple-Choice

1. **The post-Soviet Communist party is Russia is:**
    a. The democratic party of Russia
    b. The new socialist party of Russia
    c. The Communist party of the Russian Federation
    d. The Russian liberal party

2. **Mao Zedong came to power fighting the:**
    a. CCP
    b. PRI
    c. KMT
    d. USSR

3. **Which of the following was not a part of the Cultural Revolution in China?**
    a. Re-education
    b. Violence against opponents
    c. Improved, peaceful education
    d. Deportation of intellectuals

4. **Iran has a _____ Muslim majority.**
    a. Sharia
    b. Shi'ite
    c. Sunni
    d. Qu 'ran

5. **To run for the Iranian Majlis, candidates must be:**
    a. Committed to Islamic values
    b. Under 75 years old
    c. Approved by the Guardian Council
    d. All of the above

6. **Challenges for the Iranian economy include:**
    a. UN Sanctions
    b. Poor management by the conservative government
    c. Costs of war
    d. All of the above

7. **In Nigeria, which of the following is most likely to contribute to serious difficulties?**
    a. Religious conflicts
    b. Class conflicts
    c. Drug use
    d. Lack of education

8. **Which of the following countries has the most restrictive laws with regards to women?**
    a. Iran
    b. Nigeria
    c. China
    d. Mexico

9. **Which of the following is a member of NATO?**
    a. Great Britain
    b. China
    c. Iran
    d. Mexico

10. **NAFTA did what?**
    a. Improved immigration policies
    b. Encouraged trade between Mexico and the US
    c. Encouraged trade between the US and Europe
    d. Created a military alliance

11. **Which of the following is likely to favor reduced social welfare spending?**
    a. The CCP
    b. The Tories
    c. The Labour Party
    d. The Liberal Democrats

12. What is the most important defining characteristic in Nigeria?
- **a.** Ethnicity
- **b.** Religion
- **c.** Nationality
- **d.** Class

13. Margaret Thatcher was a member of which party?
- **a.** Socialist
- **b.** Conservative
- **c.** Liberal
- **d.** Labour

14. The first military coup in Nigeria occurred in:
- **a.** 1960
- **b.** 1966
- **c.** 1967
- **d.** 1970

15. Prior to 1960, Nigeria was a colony of:
- **a.** France
- **b.** Britain
- **c.** The Netherlands
- **d.** Belgium

16. The leader of Iran after the revolution was:
- **a.** Ayatollah Khomeni
- **b.** Ayatollah Ali Khamenei
- **c.** Muhammad Khatami
- **d.** Reza Shah

17. Infant mortality is highest in:
- **a.** Iran
- **b.** Mexico
- **c.** Britain
- **d.** Nigeria

18. Stalin's Five Year Plans were most successful in:
- **a.** Improving the lives of the people
- **b.** Increasing industry
- **c.** Collectivizing agriculture
- **d.** Developing international relationships

19. Under General Sani Abacha, Nigeria was:

a. Peaceful
b. Stable
c. Corrupt
d. Democratic

20. Shi'ite Muslims believe authority rests in:

a. Muhammad alone
b. Early founders of Islam
c. Modern clerics
d. The descendants of Muhammad

21. The Bracero Program:

a. Improves immigration law
b. Allows workers legal entrance to the US from Mexico
c. Is a Mexican anti-poverty program
d. Is a means of reducing ethnic differences

22. Prior to the introduction of democracy in Mexico, the nation was:

a. Corporatist
b. Pluralist
c. Limited
d. Globalized

23. Keynesianism was implemented in:

a. Nigeria
b. Britain
c. China
d. Russia

24. What is the unique or defining quality of the Iranian Revolution?

a. Communism
b. The driving force of the poor
c. Social conscience
d. Religion

25. After World War II, Iran underwent a process of:

a. Democratization
b. Globalization
c. Modernization
d. Privatization

26. The collapse in the oil market in the 1970s strongly impacted the political fates of which countries?
   a. Nigeria, Britain, Iran
   b. China, Russia, Iran
   c. China, Nigeria, Iran
   d. Iran, Nigeria, Mexico

27. The Supreme Leader:
   a. Makes laws
   b. Organizes religious celebrations
   c. Ensures that laws conform to religion
   d. Chooses clerics

28. Which group supports the clerics in enforcing laws in Iran?
   a. The Guardian Council
   b. The Supreme Leader
   c. The National Assembly
   d. The Hezbollah

29. The judicial branch of the government is responsible for censorship in which of the following?
   a. Iran
   b. Nigeria
   c. Russia
   d. China

30. Sharia law is applied in which of the following?
   a. Iran and Russia
   b. Iran and Nigeria
   c. Nigeria and Russia
   d. Great Britain and Iran

31. Women are unable to leave the country without the permission of a male relative in which country?
   a. China
   b. Russia
   c. Nigeria
   d. Iran

32. The Mexican president responsible for significant change was:
   a. Carlos Salinas
   b. Vicente Fox
   c. Ernesto Zedillo
   d. Felipe Calderon

33. Which of the following has the lowest percentage of women in the legislature?
   a. Nigeria
   b. Iran
   c. Mexico
   d. Russia

34. Drug trafficking poses the greatest challenge in which country?
   a. Nigeria
   b. Iran
   c. China
   d. Mexico

35. Prime Minister Tony Blair was a member of:
   a. The Conservative party
   b. The Labour party
   c. The Liberal democrats
   d. The Socialist party

36. Vicente Fox belonged to what political party?
   a. PRI
   b. PAN
   c. CCP
   d. PRD

37. The dominant religion in Mexico is:
   a. Catholic
   b. Protestant
   c. Muslim
   d. Indigenous

38. Mexicanization was part of:
   a. Indigenous culture
   b. The one-party system
   c. Colonial Mexico
   d. Democracy

39. What event led to the organization of the PRD in 1985?

    a. A massacre of students

    b. Drug trafficking

    c. NAFTA

    d. The Mexico City earthquake

40. Britain's Glorious Revolution occurred:

    a. In the 16th century

    b. In the 17th century

    c. In the 18th century

    d. In the 19th century

41. Under one-party rule, the judicial was subordinate to the:

    a. Executive

    b. Legislative

    c. Federal government

    d. Confederate government

42. Under the Fourth Republic in Nigeria, the press:

    a. Has lost freedom

    b. Has gained freedom

    c. Has shrunk in size

    d. Has grown in size

43. Much of the Nigerian Bureaucracy is made up of people from:

    a. The south

    b. The north

    c. The east

    d. The west

44. Sharia law is used in which part of Nigeria?

    a. North

    b. South

    c. East

    d. All of the above

45. Which of these countries was victimized by British colonization?

    a. Nigeria

    b. Iran

    c. Mexico

    d. China

46. **Which of the following relies upon its long cultural history as a key part of modern culture?**
    a. Iran
    b. Nigeria
    c. Mexico
    d. China

47. **Crosscutting social cleavages are:**
    a. Differences that divide society into different groups with regard to different issues
    b. Differences that lead to extremism
    c. Minor differences between groups
    d. Religious differences between groups

48. **Iran engaged in a long-lasting war with:**
    a. Iraq
    b. Saudi Arabia
    c. Israel
    d. The United States

49. **The majority of people in China are:**
    a. Han Chinese
    b. Mao Chinese
    c. Nepalese
    d. Buddhist

50. **Corporatism:**
    a. Offers increased numbers of interest groups
    b. Allows very few interest groups
    c. Reduces political participation
    d. Increases political participation

51. **Access to health care is the best in:**
    a. Britain
    b. China
    c. Russia
    d. Iran

52. **Which of the following nations suffers from a reduced population due to poor adult health?**
    a. Russia
    b. Britain
    c. China
    d. Mexico

53. **Which of these countries has shown the greatest economic improvement in recent years?**
    a. China
    b. Russia
    c. Britain
    d. Nigeria

54. **Economic policy includes making decisions that impact:**
    a. Trade
    b. Tariffs
    c. Imports
    d. Interest rates

55. **Which is NOT an example of a supranational organization?**
    a. The United Nations
    b. The European Union
    c. NAFTA
    d. The World Bank

Short Answer Questions

1. Describe the impact of the first Five Year Plan on agriculture in the Soviet Union.
2. Define Mexicanization and explain why it was important.
3. Define modernization and provide at least one example of modernization in one of the countries we have studied.
4. Choose one example of corruption of the democratic process and briefly explain it.
5. Explain one social cleavage in Great Britain.

Essay Questions

1. How did the Russian revolution impact Russia's role internationally, from World War I through the Cold War?

2. Name three supranational organizations and identify the role and function of each.

3. Explain the reasons for China's one-child policy, as well as the exceptions, benefits and drawbacks of this policy.

Multiple-Choice

1. **Which nation allows presidents to serve only one term?**
   a. Nigeria
   b. Mexico
   c. Iran
   d. Russia

2. **The Constitution of 1917 is:**
   a. Mexican
   b. British
   c. Russian
   d. Iranian

3. **Women in Nigeria:**
   a. Hold political power
   b. Hold power in the family
   c. Have very little power
   d. Hold significant social power

4. **A rentier state:**
   a. Has an authoritarian government
   b. Derives income from the use of natural resources by external buyers
   c. Derives income from the land
   d. Is primarily agricultural

5. **The Revolution of 1979 overthrew which government?**
   a. Mexican
   b. Persian
   c. Nigerian
   d. Russian

6. **The Revolutionary Guard is the name used for the army of which nation?**
   a. Mexico
   b. Russia
   c. Iran
   d. China

7. **Who was the first leader of the Soviet Union?**
   a. Vladimir Lenin
   b. Vladimir Putin
   c. Joseph Stalin
   d. Leon Trotsky

8. **The devolution of Britain has resulted in:**
   a. The loss of land
   b. The creation of national assemblies
   c. New courts
   d. New executive bureaucracies

9. **Reza Shah ruled:**
   a. Nigeria
   b. Iran
   c. Russia
   d. China

10. **Ethnic minorities in China:**
    a. Do not exist
    b. Live in specific, small regions
    c. Are exempt from the one-child rule
    d. Are a significant social cleavage

11. **The term "brain drain" refers to:**
    a. Intellectuals leaving Iran
    b. Intellectuals fleeing China
    c. Weak education systems
    d. Strong educational systems

12. **Guanxi refers to:**
    a. Collective farms
    b. Personal influence and networking
    c. Privatization of industry
    d. Globalization of China

13. **A first-past-the-post electoral system is likely to:**
    a. Result in a two-party system
    b. Result in a one-party system
    c. Result in a multi-party system
    d. Result in a corrupt system

14. Radical clerics in Iran favored:
   a. Economically liberal policies
   b. Social welfare programs for the poor
   c. Policies to favor the upper classes
   d. Improved education

15. China's Great Leap Forward was:
   a. A re-education program
   b. Designed to reduce objections
   c. An economic program
   d. A modernization program

16. All of the following are examples of rational-legal authority in Britain EXCEPT:
   a. Hereditary monarchy
   b. Common law
   c. The Magna Carta
   d. The Constitution of the Crown

17. Which is the most accurate description of Great Britain's political history?
   a. Violent revolution
   b. Military coups
   c. Gradual reform
   d. Economic revolution

18. The industrial revolution led to increased suffrage in which country?
   a. Britain
   b. Russia
   c. China
   d. Mexico

19. The majority of British Muslims are:
   a. From Africa
   b. From India or Pakistan
   c. Not well-integrated into society
   d. Harshly discriminated against

20. In what way does the government of Britain control the press?
   a. Through the BBC
   b. Through the courts
   c. Through a censorship board
   d. By banning political ads

21. Which of the following is descriptive of Russian political culture?

   a. Slavophile vs. westernizer

   b. Modernizer vs. democratizer

   c. Globalizer vs. slavophile

   d. Reactionary vs. conservative

22. Collectivization and industrialization were key parts of the plan of which Russian leader?

   a. Vladimir Lenin

   b. Vladimir Putin

   c. Joseph Stalin

   d. Karl Marx

23. Glasnost:

   a. Modernized the economy

   b. Encouraged criticism

   c. Increased the military

   d. Supported democracy

24. The Russian Prime Minister is:

   a. The head of the government

   b. The head of state

   c. The head of government and state

   d. The head of the legislature

25. Both Russia and Britain have seen increasing numbers of:

   a. Interest groups

   b. Political parties

   c. Muslims

   d. Reactionaries

26. As of 2014, Russia is NOT a member of which organization?

   a. The United Nations

   b. Confederation of Independent States

   c. G-8

   d. Customs Union of Belarus, Kazakhstan, and Russia

27. Neoliberalism is a feature of politics in which of these countries?
   a. Russia
   b. Mexico
   c. China
   d. Britain

28. Conflicts in Northern Ireland are largely the result of:
   a. Class differences
   b. Religion
   c. Ethnicity
   d. National identity

29. PPP measures:
   a. Average income
   b. Purchasing power
   c. Overall national wealth
   d. Average per capita wealth

30. The Mexican army is NOT:
   a. A part of the fight against drugs
   b. Well-organized
   c. Used for national defense
   d. A political policymaker

31. Corruption in Mexico is frequently related to:
   a. Oil
   b. Terrorism
   c. Immigration
   d. Drugs

32. The Zapatistas originate:
   a. In Mexico City
   b. In Northern Mexico
   c. In Eastern Mexico
   d. In the South of Mexico

33. Politically, the Zapatistas may be defined as:
   a. Revolutionaries
   b. Reformers
   c. Conservatives
   d. Reactionaries

34. Which of the following has been shared by Iran, China and Mexico?
  a. Communism
  b. Islam
  c. Authoritarianism
  d. Military Coups

35. Which of the following does NOT have a president?
  a. Russia
  b. Britain
  c. Iran
  d. Mexico

36. The highest law in Iran is:
  a. Common law
  b. Sharia law
  c. The Supreme Court
  d. The Supreme Leader

37. The Iranian economy suffered under:
  a. Reza Shah
  b. Ayatollah Khomeini
  c. Muhammad Khatami
  d. Hassan Rouhani

38. During the colonial period, the British:
  a. Encouraged differences between ethnic groups
  b. Supported Christians
  c. Supported Muslims
  d. Banned traditional practices in Nigeria

39. Which of the following was a significant struggle for parliamentary democracy in Nigeria?
  a. The lack of a majority party
  b. The inability to elect a president
  c. Colonialism
  d. International relations

40. The People's Democratic Party is:
   a. Iranian
   b. Nigerian
   c. Russian
   d. British

41. Nigeria's democracy still lacks:
   a. Freedom of speech
   b. Interest groups
   c. Civil society
   d. Free and fair elections

42. Backbenchers in the British parliament are:
   a. Members of the peerage
   b. Elected representatives without a government office
   c. Members of the majority party
   d. Elected representatives who sit in both the House of Commons and House of Lords

43. Which of the following elements of the Soviet system have been retained in Russia?
   a. Universal health care
   b. Guaranteed employment
   c. Limited class divisions
   d. Price subsidies

44. Which of the following does not provide universal health care?
   a. Nigeria
   b. Russia
   c. China
   d. Britain

45. The dominant political party in Russia is:
   a. Communist Party of the Russian Federation
   b. A Just Russia
   c. Unity
   d. United Russia

46. In early 2014, Russia annexed:
   a. Chechnya
   b. Crimea
   c. Ukraine
   d. Belarus

47. Mestizo refers to individuals who identify as:
   a. Amerindian
   b. European
   c. Of mixed Amerindian and European descent
   d. Immigrants

48. Encouraging domestic industry, rather than imports and exports is:
   a. Tariffs
   b. Gross domestic product
   c. Import substitution industrialization
   d. Privatization

49. Which of the following is NOT an ethnic group found in Nigeria
   a. Igbo
   b. Yoruba
   c. Hausa-Falani
   d. Azeri

50. When a colonial property is managed through indirect rule, the individuals governing are:
   a. Local tribespeople
   b. The military
   c. An imported colonial governor
   d. A monarch

51. Nigeria gained its independence in:
   a. 1950
   b. 1960
   c. 1966
   d. 1972

52. **Patron- client relationships are not a significant factor in government in which country?**
    a. Britain
    b. China
    c. Nigeria
    d. Russia

53. **Iran opposed the Taliban, alongside a number of other nations. Why?**
    a. The Taliban's oppressive policies
    b. The Taliban's human rights violations
    c. Their own national security
    d. Conflict between Shi'ite and Sunni Muslims

54. **Qanun refers to:**
    a. Religious law
    b. Secular law
    c. Financial law
    d. Family law

55. **During the 19th century, which nation was largely responsible for the opium trade?**
    a. China
    b. Britain
    c. Afghanistan
    d. Iran

Short Answer Questions

1. Define political participation in an authoritarian state.

2. What is the IMF? Briefly explain.

3. What is the difference between a head of state and head of government? Give at least one example of each.

4. Who is Vicente Fox?

5. Name three factors inhibiting economic growth in modern-day Iran.

Essay Questions

1. How does the existence of a constitution shape a nation? Provide at least three examples of constitutional reforms, changes or implications.

2. Based on current events, explain the cause of social violence in Nigeria today.

3. Mexico remained surprisingly stable, unlike many Latin American nations in the 20th century. Provide at least three reasons for this stability and explain why these factors were important.

1. **The Great Leap forward began in:**
   a. 1948
   b. 1957
   c. 1958
   d. 1961

2. **Deng Xiaoping is best described as:**
   a. A conservative
   b. A reformer
   c. A liberal
   d. A reactionary

3. **A socialist market economy consists of:**
   a. State-owned industry and collective agriculture
   b. Both state-owned business and private agriculture
   c. Both state-owned and privately owned businesses
   d. A market economy controlled by the state

4. **The most powerful position in China is:**
   a. Emperor
   b. General Secretary of the CCP
   c. President
   d. Prime Minister

5. **The National People's Congress of China is NOT:**
   a. An independent legislative body
   b. Designed to approve policies planned by the CCP
   c. Elected by the people
   d. A legislature in name only

6. **The bazaaris in Iran are:**
   a. The lower class
   b. The upper class elite
   c. The middle or merchant class
   d. The enforcers of Islamic law

7. **The White Revolution was an attempt to:**
    a. Encourage reform in Iran
    b. Bring about an Islamist state
    c. End the reign of the Shah
    d. End modernization and democratization

8. **Which of the following is NOT characteristic of Iran?**
    a. Nationalism
    b. Theocracy
    c. A heterogeneous culture
    d. A homogeneous culture

9. **Why did Iran's government stay in place despite the Green Revolution and later, the political forces behind the Arab Spring that swept the Middle East?**
    a. Religious fundamentalism
    b. Harsh treatment of protestors
    c. Strong democratic tradition
    d. Location

10. **Women have a growing presence in Iran in:**
    a. Politics
    b. The workplace
    c. Universities
    d. The markets

11. **Why has Iran been sanctioned by the United Nations?**
    a. War with Iraq
    b. Nuclear treaty violations
    c. Chemical warfare
    d. Human rights violations

12. **In colonial Nigeria, Britain favored:**
    a. The south
    b. The north
    c. Both the north and south
    d. Neither the north nor the south

13. Prior to the Russian revolution, the majority of the country was:
- **a.** Catholic
- **b.** Protestant
- **c.** Muslim
- **d.** Russian Orthodox

14. Under Sani Abacha in the 1990s, the government of Nigeria:
- **a.** Made economic gains
- **b.** Experienced civil war
- **c.** Was horribly corrupt
- **d.** Was a functional democracy

15. Complementary cleavages in Nigeria are:
- **a.** Class and religion
- **b.** Ethnicity and nationality
- **c.** Region and nationality
- **d.** Ethnicity and religion

16. The Nigerian military is:
- **a.** Involved in international activities in Africa
- **b.** Involved in an ongoing civil war
- **c.** Responsible for the democratic government
- **d.** Disorganized and weak in the region

17. Under which type of government are social cleavages of the least importance?
- **a.** Military
- **b.** Theocracy
- **c.** Communist
- **d.** Democratic

18. A parastatal is:
- **a.** An interest group controlled by the public
- **b.** An interest group controlled by the state
- **c.** An industry owned or partly owned by the government
- **d.** A privatized company

19. In Russian politics, "shock therapy" refers to:
- **a.** Gorbachev's plans to modernize the economy
- **b.** Yeltsin's sudden economic reforms
- **c.** Putin's annexation of the Crimea
- **d.** Russian military action against the Ukraine

20. Which of the following supports a multi-party system?

   a. First-past-the-post

   b. Presidential power

   c. Checks and balances

   d. Proportional representation

21. The Russian kulaks were:

   a. Upper class peasants

   b. Wealthy landowners

   c. Serfs

   d. Merchants

22. Nikita Khrushchev led during:

   a. The Russian Revolution

   b. World War II

   c. The Cold War

   d. World War I

23. Sinn Fein advocates for:

   a. The working class

   b. The upper class

   c. Welsh independence

   d. Irish independence

24. Radical clerics in Iran are most concerned with:

   a. The wealthy

   b. The middle class

   c. The poor

   d. Economic improvement

25. The most significant belief system impacting Chinese culture and politics is:

   a. Buddhism

   b. Confucianism

   c. Taoism

   d. Christianity

26. Ejidos describes:
   a. Collectivization of farms
   b. Communal village land used for farming
   c. An anti-poverty program
   d. A rebellion in southern Mexico

27. Dependency theory suggests that:
   a. Poverty is the result of domestic policies
   b. Poverty is the result of personal behavior
   c. Poverty is the result of global factors
   d. Poverty is the result of climatological conditions

28. In Iran, several minority religions are tolerated. These are:
   a. Christianity, Zoroastrianism, Baha'i
   b. Christianity, Judaism, Zoroastrianism
   c. Baha'i, Judaism, Zoroastrianism
   d. Islam, Christianity, Judaism

29. Which of the following countries are most likely to limit access to the internet?
   a. China, Nigeria
   b. China, Russia
   c. China, Russia, Iran
   d. Iran, Nigeria, Russia

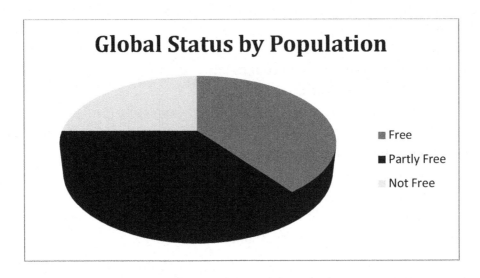

Global Status by Population

Total World Population	approx. 7,000,000,000
Population (Free)	approx. 3,000,000,000
Population (Partly Free)	approx. 2,000,000,000
Population (Not Free)	approx. 2,000,000,000

For questions 30 – 32, refer to the chart above. This chart provides an estimation of the world's population divided into approximate portions reflecting relative degrees of freedom. Here, *freedom* is determined by a country's democratic processes, political participation, civil liberties, and individual political rights.

30. Of the following, which would you expect would be *free*?
   a. Mexico
   b. Britain
   c. China
   d. Iran

31. Of the following, which would you expect would be *not free*?
   a. Mexico
   b. Russia
   c. China
   d. Britain

32. Of the following, which would you expect would be *partly free*?
    a. Iran
    b. Britain
    c. China
    d. Nigeria

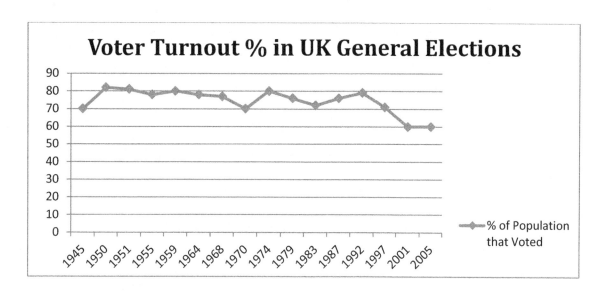

For questions 33 – 34, refer to the chart above.

33. Use this graph to answer the next two questions. What is this graph measuring?
    a. Civil society
    b. Interest groups
    c. Political participation
    d. Social cleavages

34. When was voter turnout highest?
    a. 1945
    b. 1950
    c. 1979
    d. 1951

For questions 35 – 38, refer to the map above.

35. Why would the Ukraine be a valuable territory for Russia?
   a. Historical importance
   b. Geographic importance
   c. Religious minorities
   d. Land and resources

36. A significant portion of Russia is in what biosphere, based on its northern latitude?
   a. Tundra
   b. Desert
   c. Forest
   d. Temperate

37. Russia's largest neighbor to the south is:
   a. Kazakhstan
   b. Ukraine
   c. China
   d. Mongolia

38. Large portions of Russia are:
   a. Highly developed
   b. Minimally populated
   c. Heavily populated
   d. Agricultural

39. The Tiananmen Square protest and massacre occurred in:
   a. Beijing
   b. Shanghai
   c. Nanchang
   d. Fuzhou

40. The nomenklatura is:
   a. A member of the Communist party
   b. A list of Communist party elite
   c. A ballot for Communist party elections
   d. A committee in the Communist party

41. The Duma is:
   a. The Russian legislature
   b. The Russian executive
   c. The Russian head of government
   d. The Russian head of state

42. Karl Marx:
   a. Led the Russian Revolution
   b. Led the Red Army
   c. Wrote the Communist Manifesto
   d. Wrote the Russian constitution of 1993

43. Special economic zones in China:
   a. Encourage domestic investment
   b. Offer entrepreneurship training
   c. Offer improved education
   d. Encourage foreign investment

44. Why is China desirable to foreign investors?
   a. Quality of goods
   b. Price of goods
   c. State control of business
   d. Free market economy

45. The indigenous people of Mexico live primarily in the:
   a. North
   b. South
   c. Throughout the country
   d. In the southernmost tip of the country

46. The Nigerian civil war in 1967 focused on:
   a. The Republic of Biafra
   b. Tensions between north and south
   c. Religious disputes
   d. Control of the country

47. PEMEX is:
   a. A Mexican political party
   b. A Mexican petroleum company
   c. A Mexican interest group
   d. A trade agreement

48. What is the correct definition of the word "jihad"?
   a. Holy war
   b. Struggle
   c. Faith
   d. Loyalty

49. A structural adjustment program is designed to:
   a. Stabilize democracy
   b. Reduce social cleavages
   c. Repay debt
   d. Improve conditions for the people

50. The IMF:
   a. Manages international debt
   b. Provides low-cost loans to developing countries
   c. Provides support to the UN
   d. Provides loans to developed countries

51. In 2014, Russia was forced out of what supranational organization?
   a. The IMF
   b. G-8
   c. The UN
   d. The EU

52. As of 2014, who is president of Nigeria?
   a. Goodluck Jonathan
   b. Umaru Yar'adua
   c. Sani Abacha
   d. Olusegun Obasanjo

53. Which of the countries studied are most likely to maintain good diplomatic relations and be allies?

    a. Britain and Iran

    b. Britain, Russia and China

    c. Nigeria, Britain and Iran

    d. Russia, Iran and China

54. The Household Responsibility System allows farmers:

    a. To control the land they work

    b. To work on collective farms

    c. To own the land they work

    d. To have children without permission

55. Township and Village Enterprises:

    a. Encourage a market economy

    b. Support the lower classes

    c. Provide jobs in underemployed regions

    d. All of the above

Short Answer Questions

1. Explain the difference between a corporatist and pluralist system. Identify one country that was formerly corporatist, but now favors a pluralist approach to interest groups.

2. Identify one nation at risk for genocide and explain the social cleavages contributing to that risk.

3. Explain which organization approves candidates for election to the Maljis and how this impacts the political process.

4. Identify one country that would be defined as a welfare state and briefly explain the social programs associated with this.

5. Name three ways in which colonial occupation contributed to the instability of Nigeria.

Essay Questions

1. Identify and explain at least two conflicts caused by ethnic social cleavages.

2. Discuss the process of modernization in China today, including its impact on the global economy.

3. Describe the Iranian revolution of 1979, including at least three specific ways in which religion shaped this revolution.

Answers I

Multiple-Choice

1.	A	29.	B
2.	C	30.	A
3.	B	31.	B
4.	C	32.	B
5.	C	33.	C
6.	C	34.	C
7.	B	35.	D
8.	C	36.	B
9.	D	37.	B
10.	B	38.	B
11.	D	39.	C
12.	C	40.	A
13.	B	41.	D
14.	C	42.	D
15.	D	43.	C
16.	B	44.	A
17.	A	45.	C
18.	A	46.	D
19.	D	47.	A
20.	C	48.	D
21.	C	49.	C
22.	D	50.	C
23.	A	51.	B
24.	B	52.	B
25.	C	53.	B
26.	D	54.	B
27.	B	55.	B
28.	C		

Short Answer

1. How did the collectivization of agriculture impact rural China?

Prior to the Communist revolution in China, the land was farmed by individual households. While there was a large population, there was also an adequate food supply. Collectivization occurred in two phases. During the first, small family farms were collectivized into communes of around 250 families. During the second phase, these were gathered into much larger communes with thousands of families. Originally, the farmers ate communal meals in a large gathering hall; however, production fell dramatically under collectivization. Eventually famine resulted, leading to a large number of deaths. Once it was clear that collectivization had failed, farms returned to household responsibility. In this system, the land was still collectively owned, but individual households worked the land and were free to do what they pleased with surplus after meeting quotas.

2. Which of these countries chooses to embrace past culture, even though there are substantial differences between that culture and the modern nation? Identify the country and briefly explain.

Iran actively integrates historical, Persian culture into the modern state, as well as Islamic history. Very early in written history, this region saw the beginning of culture, including art and religion. In the classical world Persia was, traditionally, a capital of great learning, with substantial historical significance. After Muhammad founded Islam, Iran was home to a number of Islamic dynasties, including the Safavid dynasty. Iran is a Shi'ite Muslim state, believing that the most important teachings of Islam are passed down through the direct descent of the Prophet. These links to the past have helped to add legitimacy to the theocracy of modern-day Iran, and serve to appeal to the middle classes and the educated, who are most likely to resist the current regime.

3. **What is Glasnost?**

In the late 1980s, under the leadership of Mikhail Gorbachev, reform began in the Soviet Union. The countries of Eastern Europe were rapidly changing, moving from their post-war Communist governments to new and modern democracies. In response, the tight control of the Communist party lessened .Glasnost encouraged far more freedom of speech, including the ability to criticize the government, than had ever been allowed before in the Communist Soviet Union. Along with economic reforms, these changes paved the way for the eventual collapse of the Soviet Union and creation of the Russian Federation.

4. **Define globalization and give at least one example of how it has impacted the countries studied.**

Globalization refers to creating an international or global community. Supranational organizations with significant power are the best example of this globalization. The largest supranational organization is the United Nations or UN. The UN serves as a peacekeeping organization, negotiating disputes and even engaging in coalition-based peacekeeping action when necessary, as has occurred in Bosnia-Herzegovina and Somalia. Currently, the United Nations has sanctioned Iran. Sanctions are economic measures, rather than military ones. These are designed to encourage the country to change its behavior by causing economic challenges. In this case, Iran has engaged in weapons planning and design, as well as nuclear testing.

5. **How has privatization impacted Communist and post-Communist countries? Identify at least one example.**

Privatization is the process of selling state owned factories or resources to private citizens. It typically occurs during the transition from a Communist economic system to a free-market system, as seen in both Russia and China and is a part of modernization. In Russia, state-owned companies were sold off quite rapidly, during a short period referred to as economic "shock therapy" under Boris Yeltsin. This resulted in a small number of individuals owning a large amount of former state property and created an oligarchy of these wealthy and influential individuals. In China, the transition to a market-based economy has occurred much more slowly, as first individuals were allowed to own companies and gradually, assets were privatized, either in full or in part.

Essay

1. **Explain the international response to recent events within Russia, including the Chechen rebellion and the annexation of the Ukraine.**

   Russia is a relatively young democracy, with a constitution dating to 1993. The early years of democracy were particularly corrupt, under the leadership of Boris Yeltsin. While the Russian electoral process is now rather stable, Russian political actions, as well as military actions, suggest that Russia is not as removed from its dominating past as once thought. The Russian Federation, under President Vladimir Putin, is progressively leaning toward the right in a movement that is, at best, described as conservative, and at worst, reactionary.

   Chechnya has sought independence from the Russian Federation for some time, leading to war in the early 1990s and into 2000. Russian troops did significant damage to the country during the course of the war. Chechnya lost and remained part of the Russian Federation; however, small-scale insurgency continues. This conflict also carries with it a religious component, as, while much of Russia is non-religious, Chechnya is largely Muslim and the insurgency movement is dominantly so.

   While the conflict with Chechnya was a domestic one and largely ignored by the international community, the same cannot be said of a more recent conflict. In early 2014, Russia annexed Crimea. The Crimean peninsula was previously part of the Ukraine, but this ethnically Russian region was administered largely autonomously. In February 2014, Russia annexed the Crimea, crossing the borders of the Ukraine to do so. The Ukraine was in the midst of a political crisis, enabling this action. While Crimea approved the annexation, it was not handled legally or with respect to the borders of the Ukraine.

   The United Nations condemned this action and Russia was removed from the supranational organization the G-8, which will now meet as the G-7. Other supranational organizations, including the EU, have also reaffirmed the sovereignty of the Ukraine and condemned Russia's actions. Russia's actions are seen by many in the international community as a sign of growing nationalism and militarism by Vladimir Putin and his administration. The progressive trend toward right-wing politics in Russia has drawn attention to the nation's politics, actions and possible future decisions.

2. Identify three ways in which the history of Iran or Islam is important for modern day Iran and how these have shaped the state.

At the time of the 1979 Revolution, Iran was a vital, lively and surprisingly western culture that embraced its historical past, including the long history of the region, from very ancient times through the Persian Empire and the prominence of the region along the Silk Road. The Revolution initially tried to remove all of those aspects from the culture of Iran, emphasizing only Islamic history, for instance, the importance of the Safavid Dynasty. Today, the theocratic government of Iran works to integrate an appreciation for both Iranian and Islamic history into the culture of modern Iran.

The most fundamental aspect of Islamic history is found in the official state religion of Iran, Shi'itism. Shi'itism believes that authority comes from the direct, physical descent of the Prophet Muhammad. As such, history and tracing the lineage of the Prophet is of essential importance to the state.

Iran celebrates its Persian history not in a religious sense, but a cultural one. Tourism is encouraged, particularly with countries friendly to Iran and Islam. The historic pre-Islamic sites are accepted, cared for and embraced as a part of the region's history, with no conflict with Islam. Early Islamic sites are also treated with great respect in the country. The change in attitudes toward Persian history occurred later in the revolutionary government, in response to the desires of the people.

The Safavid Dynasty is frequently mentioned in discussions of Iranian religious history. The Safavids created a Shi'ite empire, in clear opposition to the Sunni Muslim-led empires around Iran. The 1979 Revolution drew inspiration from this period, hoping to return Iran to its status at this time. This is a significant time for both Iran and Islam, making it an especially important part of the cultural history of modern day Iran.

This interest in culture and history helps to legitimize the Iranian regime. It becomes, through this use of history, a part of a continuing tradition of a powerful state and Shi'ite government.

3. **Compare and contrast at least two examples of democratic reform with two examples of revolution, democratic or not.**

Reform and revolution are distinctly different, even when the conclusions are relatively similar. Reform is a gradual and typically peaceful process. Revolution is a sudden and usually violent one. While the eventual goals of both reformers and revolutionaries may be similar, the means they choose to use are often very different.

Democratic reform has occurred in both Great Britain and Mexico, albeit over very different timetables. In Britain, reform was quite slow, occurring progressively and gradually over hundreds of years in small steps. Only during and after the industrial revolution did the pace of reform increase rather dramatically, leading to universal suffrage relatively quickly, as well as the creation of a modern executive branch of government. In Mexico, the trappings of democracy were present with the creation of the constitution in 1917; however, the state remained authoritarian. Beginning in the middle of the 1980s, things began to change. The people spoke out, the media began to take an active role in exposing the corruption in the government and new political parties grew. From the initial response to the tragic earthquake in Mexico City in 1985 to the elections of 1990, the state transitioned entirely from an authoritarian government to a democratic one. Neither of these reform movements saw substantial violence and both grew out of the efforts of the people to advocate for political change. In both Mexico and Britain, these reforms led to an overall improvement in quality of life for the people of the nation.

Revolution, too, typically comes from the efforts of the people to advocate change; however, in the modern world, revolution has not customarily led to democracy. Two of the most significant revolutions of the 20th century, in China and Russia, led to Communism. In both cases, these revolutions were accompanied by significant military action. In Russia, the Red Army overthrew the government, while in China the CCP engaged in battled with the KMT. Once in place, the revolutionary government continued to act violently toward their citizens. In Russia, any opposition was crushed through the action of Stalin and his government, culminating in the Holodomor or engineered famine in 1932 and 1933. Similar events occurred in China to eliminate resistance, including the re-education camps or labor camps used to silence dissidents and the famine that followed the Great Leap Forward of 1959-1961. Neither the Russian Revolution nor the Chinese Revolution significantly improved the lives of the people and both, in fact, led to large numbers of deaths.

This minimal analysis suggests that radical revolutionary activity can be connected with instability and violence. While not every revolution has resulted in this, it has been true for many, even those striving for democracy, like the French Revolution. Reform can produce change, but it is not as rapid and may not, initially, be as extreme. It does, however, offer substantially less risk of violence and a greater chance of stability.

Answers II

Multiple-Choice

1.	C	29.	A
2.	C	30.	B
3.	C	31.	D
4.	B	32.	B
5.	D	33.	A
6.	D	34.	D
7.	A	35.	B
8.	A	36.	B
9.	A	37.	A
10.	B	38.	B
11.	B	39.	D
12.	A	40.	B
13.	B	41.	A
14.	B	42.	B
15.	B	43.	A
16.	A	44.	A
17.	D	45.	A
18.	B	46.	A
19.	C	47.	A
20.	D	48.	A
21.	B	49.	A
22.	A	50.	B
23.	B	51.	A
24.	D	52.	A
25.	C	53.	A
26.	D	54.	D
27.	C	55.	C
28.	D		

1. **Describe the impact of the first Five Year Plan on agriculture in the Soviet Union.**

   Agriculture was collectivized during the first Five Year Plan. Traditionally, in Russia, much of the land was owned by large land owners and worked by serfs. There was also a class of more educated, lower-class landowners, called kulags, which could be defined as the Russian middle class of this time. Under the Five Year Plan, all land was under state control. During this time, the entirety of the kulag class was destroyed by Stalin. Furthermore, the state controls were manipulated to trigger a large-scale famine in the Ukraine, the richest agricultural land in the Soviet Union. Weather conditions led to a poor harvest and state mandated quotas were not adjusted to allow for food for the workers. Millions in the Ukraine died during this time.

2. **Define Mexicanization and explain why it was important.**

   Mexicanization celebrated Mexican culture during the middle of the 20th century. This was vibrant, lively, colorful and distinct. Mexican culture is best defined as mestizo culture, incorporating both elements of Spanish culture and traditional indigenous cultures. While Mexicanization had a number of different aspects, it is best remembered for large scale visual artwork, like mural painting. These large public paintings served as propaganda, sharing a social message about the Mexican worker and supporting the work of the Mexican government in creating a stable country for their people. It had a message, helped to create a Mexican identity, and encouraged unity among the people of Mexico.

3. **Define modernization and provide at least one example of modernization in one of the countries we have studied.**

Modernization is progressive movement from a nationalized or government-owned economy to a capitalist system or free market economy. China, today, is an excellent example of modernization and illustrates how modernization and democratization do not have to go hand-in-hand. Modernization in China began with an allowance for private ownership of companies, and has progressively moved toward private ownership of various means of production, as well as household responsibility for agriculture. Today, towns and villages are encouraged to improve their economies through the creation of new businesses and foreign countries are given incentives to build factories in China. China has become one of the most vibrant world economies, actively growing and playing a major role in the production of consumer goods.

4. **Choose one example of corruption of the democratic process and briefly explain it.**

The democratic process is, ideally, free of corruption; however, this is not often true. In Nigeria, repeated elections have illustrated how very corrupt the democratic process can be. Voters have been threatened or cajoled, either to vote for a particular candidate or not to vote at all. An inability to safely cast a vote is one form of corruption; however, corruption can also easily occur at other points in the electoral process. For instance, votes can be lost or illegally created, giving a victory to one candidate over another when the will of the people went a different direction. In order for a nation to be considered a democracy, it must have free, fair and competitive elections. Corruption in the electoral process damages those elections and thus, the democracy.

5. **Explain one social cleavage in Great Britain.**

While there are a number of social cleavages in Britain, nationalism is the clearest of those. Great Britain is made up of England, Wales, Scotland and Northern Ireland. While Wales and Scotland have retained a national identity with relative peace in recent decades, continuing violence in Northern Ireland is the result of the social cleavage of nationality in Britain. Today, the nation is undergoing devolution in response to this social cleavage. The state has created national assemblies in Scotland, Wales, and Northern Ireland, allowing the people of these individual nations legislative powers at home, rather than being fully under the control of the English Parliament. This social cleavage is further emphasized by movements to preserve and teach in the native language of each country, and by religious differences between nationalities, particularly Ireland and England.

Essay

1. **How did the Russian revolution impact Russia's role internationally, from World War I through the Cold War?**

The Russian Revolution in 1917 altered Russia's international role in significant ways. Traditionally, Russia had occupied a rather unusual place, on the cusp of both Europe and Asia, and somewhat removed from European politics. During the 19th century, Russia began to play a larger role in European politics and European culture became more influential in Russia. By the early 20th century, Russia was relatively closely allied with Britain and France, standing against German alliances with Austria-Hungary and Italy. Russia entered World War I along with its allies; however, the Russian army suffered horrific defeats, contributing to the Revolution.

After the Revolution, Russia ended its involvement in World War I, accepting German terms of surrender. While the war continued elsewhere, Russia focused on its own needs. After Lenin's death, there was a conflict over leadership. Leon Trotsky, the head of the Red Army, believed that the Communists had a responsibility to work toward change internationally, while Stalin believed that stabilizing and improving Russia was the first priority. Stalin took leadership of the Soviet Union and Russia played relatively little role in the international world during the 1920s and 1930s. Domestically, this period was marked by significant violence, including Stalin's campaigns against the kulags and planned, organized famine in the Ukraine.

In 1941, Adolf Hitler initiated Operation Barbarossa, invading the Soviet Union. The Soviet Union, under Joseph Stalin, now took a much more active role in the world, participating as one of the Allies in World War II. Eventually, Soviet troops were responsible for taking Berlin, marking the final end of Hitler's war. The Soviets played a significant role in the division of land after the war and gained control, in this process, over Eastern Europe, installing Communist governments.

The years after World War II are identified as the Cold War. Both the United States and Soviet Union had nuclear arms and were prepared to use them. This was a time of division and tension, with little room for middle ground or compromise. Europe was divided by the Soviet Union, with limited access to travel or trade between the countries. The countries of Western Europe united to form NATO during this time, while Eastern Europe formed the Eastern Bloc, in opposition to NATO. This conflict continued until the gradual fall of Communism, including revolutions throughout Eastern Europe, the fall of the Berlin Wall, installed in the 1960s, and the eventual collapse of Communism in the Soviet Union in 1993 and creation of the Russian Federation.

2. Name three supranational organizations and identify the role and function of each.

Supranational organizations are international organizations involving multiple nations working together for a common goal. There are a number of supranational organizations in the world today, some focused on a specific region and others impacting the world as a whole. These organizations are a part of the globalization of the world and are typically particularly favored by democratic governments and free market economies.

The United Nations, created after World War II, is the most significant supranational organization. The United Nations goal is to preserve national borders and maintain peace internationally. Nearly all countries are part of the UN, with only three of the 196 nations in the world not member states. The United Nations has a number of powers, including investigative and peacekeeping. As an entity, the United Nations can vote to sanction a nation economically or has the ability to send forces into a country to prevent genocide, maintain borders and help support peace.

The EU or European Union is another example of a supranational organization. The European Union is a union of European states that have agreed to broad linkages between nations. Many countries in the EU now share the same currency, the Euro and individuals may pass between nations with ease, living and working in another EU country without difficulty. The EU is perhaps the best example of globalization, as this union is progressively moving toward a single European nation, rather than a number of individual nations within Europe. Conflicts do arise among member states, with disagreement over British involvement in Iraq a particular recent issue.

The IMF or International Monetary Fund is also a supranational organization, this one with a much more specific cause. The IMF, managed by developed nations and headquartered in Washington D.C., funds development in developing nations. As such, it is able to encourage the formation of free market economies and place conditions upon the nation. While these low-cost funds can dramatically improve the economy of a developing country, they also lead to debt. Repayment terms may be difficult, as is the case in Nigeria, and austerity programs can be damaging to the people of a nation. The goal of the IMF is economic development and overall economic improvement; however, these goals are less easily managed when government corruption and mismanagement occurs.

In an increasingly global world and global economy, the importance of supranational organizations is likely to increase. These organizations serve as a sort of check and balance internationally, providing the global community with the ability to respond to domestic issues.

3. Explain the reasons for China's one-child policy, as well as the exceptions, benefits and drawbacks of this policy.

Faced with a growing population and concerns about overpopulation, land and food supplies, China instituted a one child per family policy in the 1970s. This policy allowed couples to have only a single child, in most circumstances, quite dramatically reducing the birth rate. While it has successfully reduced population growth, this policy has also caused a number of substantial problems.

The one-child policy was successfully implemented through town and city supervision of health care, contraception, marriage and child-bearing permissions. These reduced accidental pregnancies and supported the government's goal of reduced birth rate. While contraception, later marriage and family planning were all part of this plan, it also included, in some cases, forced abortion and sterilization. Substantial fines were levied for additional children born without permission.

Even early in its history, there were a number of exceptions to the one-child policy. Some families could have a second child if their first was a girl or was born with a disability. Ethnic minorities could have more than one child or were exempt from childbearing limits altogether. Rural families and families who had lost a child were also often allowed a second child. Wealthier families sometimes left the country to bear a second or third child, as children born outside of China were not included in the limits. Today, in response to population challenges, the policy is changing, with more families allowed a second child than ever before.

The one-child policy has caused a number of significant social problems. China is now faced with a much smaller than typical young adult population, responsible for caring for an aging population. This poses a substantial economic problem, even in a thriving economy. Chinese culture with its traditional Confucian preference for male children has led to a seriously disparate sex ratio, with significantly more men than women. This phenomenon, sometimes referred to as "missing girls" is likely the result of sex-selective abortion and abandonment. This is causing problems for young men, unable to marry, and is likely to impact the population further in the long run.

These challenges are the primary reason for changes to the one-child law. While China achieved reduced population growth, it did so at the price of its future. With a smaller young population and significant disparity in the sex ratios, even with current changes to the one-child policy, it is likely that these demographic problems will continue for some time.

Answers III

Multiple-Choice

1. A	29. B
2. A	30. D
3. B	31. D
4. B	32. D
5. B	33. A
6. C	34. C
7. A	35. B
8. B	36. B
9. B	37. B
10. C	38. A
11. A	39. A
12. B	40. B
13. A	41. D
14. B	42. B
15. C	43. A
16. A	44. A
17. C	45. D
18. A	46. B
19. B	47. C
20. D	48. C
21. A	49. D
22. C	50. A
23. B	51. B
24. B	52. A
25. C	53. D
26. C	54. B
27. B	55. B
28. D	

Short Answer

1. **Define political participation in an authoritarian state.**

   Political participation is challenging in an authoritarian state. Typically, individuals either lack the right to vote or lack the right to cast a meaningful vote. Common means of participation in a democratic government are inaccessible. Individuals may participate in the political system through rallies and protests; however, they do take some risks along with this, as sometimes violent action may result. Other forms of protest, including spreading information or helping allow access to information, may also serve as a form of participation in the political process. In the case of China, student protestors were killed when military troops opened fire in Tiananmen Square in 1985.

2. **What is the IMF? Briefly explain.**

   The IMF is the International Monetary Fund. This fund, organized and managed internationally, is designed to provide low-interest loans to developing countries. These loans can help to fund economic development of all sorts, from natural resource exploitation to agriculture. The IMF does require that countries modernize, accepting free market economics, in order to be eligible for loans. Loans are conditional, including a variety of terms, like structural adjustment. These loans are designed to improve the global economy and are a part of overall globalization as one of many supranational organizations.

3. **What is the difference between a head of state and head of government? Give at least one example of each.**

   While the head of state and head of government can be a single position, in some countries, they are two separate posts. In Great Britain, the monarch is the head of state. This position serves several ceremonial functions, including greeting diplomats and formally opening Parliament. The head of government serves a functional purpose, leading the state and serving as the head of the executive branch of government. In Britain, this is the Prime Minister. In nations with both a president and a prime minister, one is typically head of state and the other head of government.

4. **Who is Vicente Fox?**

Vicente Fox was president of Mexico from 2000 to 2006. Fox was a businessman, affiliated with the Mexican political party PAN. As president, Vicente Fox was not remarkable. He made no significant or substantial achievements. He was, however, and most importantly, the first opposition candidate elected president in Mexico for over 70 years. The election of Fox marks the final end of the one-party system in Mexico and the beginning of a true, competitive democracy.

5. **Name three factors inhibiting economic growth in modern-day Iran.**

There are a number of factors causing economic challenges in Iran, all originating since the revolution. First, the government put into place following the revolution, led by the Ayatollah Khomeini, had little interest in economic issues and even active distaste for business. This led to mismanagement of the nation's wealth. Second, Iran engaged in a long, drawn-out and costly war with Iraq. Finally, weapons programs in Iran have led to significant United Nations sanctions. These economic sanctions are designed to hurt the economy in the hopes of changing the nation's behavior.

Essay

1. **How does the existence of a constitution shape a nation? Provide at least three examples of constitutional reforms, changes or implications.**

   A constitution can dramatically change the structure of government or help to create long-lasting reform within a government. Constitutions vary, from the gradually accumulated Constitution of the Crown in Great Britain, to the more formal constitutions of Mexico and Russia. The strength of a constitution depends upon both the text of the constitution and the government.

   In Britain, the constitution developed slowly and progressively through a series of documents, laws and policies. This was a peaceful and stable process, compared to the struggles of many other countries. In Britain, the first document in the Constitution of the Crown, the Magna Carta, created parliament. Later documents, like the Bill of Rights, increased the rights of parliament, while legislative changes eventually resulted in the role of the monarch as ceremonial head of state, , and the prime minister as the head of government, taking all executive functions.

   Mexico passed a constitution in 1917. This created a stable government, but not a democratic one. While the constitution allowed for elections, these elections were not fair or competitive. The constitution did serve to reduce the potential for significant civil war or rebellion and formed a foundation for the eventual true democracy that developed in the late 1980s and early 1990s with competitive elections and an end to the one-party system. In this case, the constitution provided some benefits, but was only one small step on a path to democracy.

   Russia passed a constitution in 1993, after the downfall of the Communist party. The Russian constitution created a framework for an organized multi-party government; however, did not produce a liberal democratic society, nor were adequate checks and balances in place. This constitution is fundamentally rather weak, and under Vladimir Putin, power has progressively been consolidated in the office of the president. This has reduced the value of the constitution and allowed for a number of reforms reducing the civil rights of the Russian people.

   The constitution is only as valuable as the government protecting it and committed to it. While Britain's democracy developed with a collection of documents loosely organized as a constitution, it thrived. Other nations, even with a well-written and thorough constitution, were unable to achieve a stable democracy. In the case of Russia, the corruption remaining within the country and lack of commitment to the democratic process illustrates a state progressively returning to a more authoritarian form of government, regardless of the existence of a constitution.

2. **Based on current events, explain the cause of social violence in Nigeria today.**

Nigeria today is considered to be at risk for genocide. Acts of violence, and particularly violence against civilians, are becoming commonplace in the northeastern part of Nigeria. Villages have been massacred and large-scale kidnappings have occurred. Committed primarily by a militant group called Boko Haram, these acts are the result of longstanding ethnic and religious social cleavages, colonial history and contemporary politics.

The nation of Nigeria is made up of a remarkably large number of diverse tribes, each with its own culture, language and history. This history included relationships between the tribes, both positive and negative, but individuals within Nigeria have consistently felt a very strong identification with a tribe, rather than as a citizen of the nation.

The tribes of Nigeria are not only divided by culture and history, but also by religion. In the south, Christianity, brought by European missionaries, is dominant. In the northern part of the country, the majority of the tribes are Islamic. A relatively small percentage of the population continues to practice native African religions. Religious tensions between Muslims and Christians have contributed to the conflicts in Nigeria. While the leader of Boko Haram claims to be Muslim, Muslim leaders in Nigeria have publicly denounced his violent activities.

Under the British colonial government, the south, and Christian tribes, were favored over the north. Christian missionaries built schools and created an educational system that is contrary to the values of radical Islamic militants. Furthermore, tribes in the south were allowed more self-governance than those in the north, contributing to resentment. The terrorist organization, Boko Haram, has already begun to target schools, particularly those teaching girls, for acts of violence.

The modern Nigerian state is formally a democracy, but allegations of corruption are common. The country has had difficulty developing a functional government because of the diversity of ethnic and religious issues in the country. The lack of a stable government has created an environment that allows for terrorist groups and activity, like that of Boko Haram. Radical leaders affiliated with Boko Haram have claimed that the government has not only discriminated against members of the Hausa-Falani tribe, but has engaged in ethnic cleansing and substantial violence against Muslims in the region.

The culmination of these tensions is a nation in near-crisis. International authorities, including developed nations, have offered assistance in combating violence in Nigeria; however, solutions remain unclear.

3. **Mexico remained surprisingly stable, unlike many Latin American nations in the 20th century. Provide at least three reasons for this stability and explain why these factors were important.**

While Mexico experienced some challenges in the 20th century, they were substantially less than the military coup d'etats, violence and civil war that wracked much of Central and South America during this time. In fact, the Mexican government was, if authoritarian, stable throughout the 20th century and even through the transition to democracy near the end of the century.

The Mexican constitution dates to 1917 and provides for a clear executive, legislative and judicial branch. It addressed basic rights and responsibilities, as well as set forth election law, term limits and the rights of various regions. While this document was based on the United States' constitution, it failed in one clear regard. Throughout much of the century, there was a single, dominant political party, the PRI. The PRI set the agenda for the nation, made the laws and decided which interest groups were allowed in Mexico. This was not a democratic government, but an authoritarian one. It was, however, an authoritarian government controlled by a group, rather than an individual, producing less regime change and instability.

During the course of the 20th century, Mexico made several economic improvements, including the discovery of oil reserves. A thriving economy reduces the risk for revolution and calls for reform. The economic boom that occurred during this time helped to lend legitimacy to the government.

Finally, the government was an effective propagandist. Mexicanization created and celebrated a Mexican identity, identifying the Mexican people with hard work, loyalty and other virtues that would benefit an authoritarian government.

The stability of the Mexican government throughout the 20th century contributed to a surprisingly peaceful and easy transition from an authoritarian government to a democratic one. Gradual reforms, including additional freedom of the press, along with protests by the people, allowed new political parties to emerge, begin to win elections and find success in the Mexican government, finally creating, from the constitution of 1917, a democracy.

Answers IV

Multiple-Choice

1. C	29. C
2. B	30. B
3. C	31. C
4. B	32. A
5. A	33. C
6. C	34. B
7. A	35. D
8. C	36. A
9. A	37. D
10. C	38. B
11. B	39. A
12. A	40. B
13. D	41. A
14. C	42. C
15. D	43. D
16. A	44. B
17. C	45. B
18. C	46. A
19. B	47. B
20. D	48. B
21. A	49. C
22. C	50. B
23. D	51. B
24. C	52. A
25. B	53. D
26. B	54. A
27. C	55. D
28. B	

Short Answer

1. **Explain the difference between a corporatist and pluralist system. Identify one country that was formerly corporatist, but now favors a pluralist approach to interest groups.**

   In a corporatist system, the state must approve all interest groups. There are relatively few groups favored by the state, limiting the potential for advocacy or economic gain. In a pluralist system, all interest groups have access to the same resources. Prior to democratization, under the one-party system, Mexico was a corporatist state. Only a few interest groups were allowed, and participation in those was limited. This reduced competition for government contracts or legislative change. Today, a wide variety of groups exist, advocating for various political, economic and social causes.

2. **Identify one nation at risk for genocide and explain the social cleavages contributing to that risk.**

   Today, Nigeria is at serious risk of genocide. By definition, genocide requires an ethnic, national or religious division, with one group targeted by another. Ongoing and escalating violence by northern groups, including the organization Boko Haram, against Christians from the south, including the Igbo, poses significant risks to this population. Ethnic divisions between tribal groups, like the Hausa-Falani and the Igbo, are the most significant social cleavage in this population; however, there is a complementary cleavage. Religion and ethnicity are closely linked in Nigeria, with Islam widespread in the north and Christianity in the south.

3. **Explain which organization approves candidates for election to the Maljis and how this impacts the political process.**

   The Maljis is the Iranian legislative body or national assembly. This is only one part of the Iranian government, and while there is a functional multi-party system in Iran, all candidates must be approved by the Guardian Council. The Guardian Council is a clerical body that serves a number of executive functions, but also must vet all candidates for the Maljis. Candidates must be shown to be devout Muslims, living in accordance with Sharia law, in order to be approved for election to the Maljis. The approval process reduces the possibility of radical or liberal candidates, as they can simply be eliminated before they reach the ballot. This helps to produce a legislative body in accordance with Muslim law.

4. **Identify one country that would be defined as a welfare state and briefly explain the social programs associated with this.**

Great Britain is typically considered to be a welfare state. Following World War II, Britain embraced the ideas of John Keynes. Keynesian economics favored caring for the people of a nation, job creation and social services, even when a nation had to go into debt to afford those programs. The social welfare programs created in Britain include the National Health Service, pension programs, cash payments for the poor, disability payments, and job assistance. These services are designed to care for the weakest members of society, but also to help equalize society, providing for the basic needs of all people in the hopes of improving the society as a whole.

5. **Name one significant way in which colonial occupation contributed to the instability of Nigeria.**

Colonial occupation for many years contributed to the challenges and struggles of modern Nigeria. The most significant problem with the colonial occupation was the progressive favoritism of the south. Colonial official favored the south and the tribes in the south over the north, offering them benefits and instituting improved education in this portion of the country. Bureaucracies were largely made up of Christian southerners. The north was ignored and less developed under the colonial government, increasing the tension and conflict between the two. The post-colonial government continued to favor tribes from the south. This conflict continues today, as northern tribes have begun engaging in ongoing and aggressive action against southern tribes.

Essay

1. **Identify and explain at least two conflicts caused by ethnic social cleavages.**

    Ethnic social cleavages are common source of conflict, both historically and today. These cleavages are more pronounced in some nations than in others. Some countries, like Great Britain, are ethnically homogeneous, while others manage ethnic cleavages without substantial tension. In other countries, ethnic conflicts pose a far greater difficulty. In Nigeria, ethnic conflicts have been at the root of substantial violence, while in Mexico, ethnic conflicts in the south have caused some amount of political disruption.

    In Nigeria, ethnic conflicts have caused significant problems for many years. Nigeria is home to a number of different tribes, each with its own culture. These tribes, while sometimes allied, have often come into conflict. In the past, this conflict was exacerbated by favoritism on the part of the British colonial government. Ethnic differences led to the Biafran civil war and today, to acts of terrorism in the northeastern part of the country. Ethnic differences in Nigeria are exacerbated by a complementary cleavage: religion. The dominant tribes are from the southern part of the country and are Christian, while the northern tribes are more commonly Muslim.

    Ethnic social cleavages are somewhat less pronounced in Mexico, but are also exacerbated by colonial history. In the case of Mexico, that is the history of Spanish colonization. While the majority of people in Mexico have both European and indigenous heritage, identifying as Mestizos, there is a relatively large minority that identifies as native or Amerindian. The Amerindian population is more significant in the southern part of the country. In the south, these people organized forming the EZLN, sometimes called the Zapatistas. This group actively resists the Mexican government, but has largely maintained a strategy of civil resistance. The EZLN, headquartered in Chiapas, continue to work for indigenous rights, gaining progressive support for their reforms.

    These two examples of ethnic cleavage have had substantially different results. In Nigeria, violence is escalating, frequently involves civilians and is garnering some amount of international attention. In Mexico, the EZLN is operating largely peacefully, gaining power and prestige through successful and thoughtful civil action, rather than violence.

2. **Discuss the process of modernization in China today, including its impact on the global economy.**

After the failure of the Great Leap Forward, progressive small steps have been taken toward modernization in China. Modernization does not imply democratization, as these steps have not resulted in a true say in the government or additional civil rights for the people of China. Modernization has provided aspects of a free market economy in China, including the ability to start businesses, accumulate personal wealth and mark class distinctions.

The first step in the modernization process was the ability to start businesses privately. The government did not privatize industry at this point, but allowed for entrepreneurship. This allowed for additional steps toward modernization. These industries worked with foreign businesses and had to be able to deal, economically, with those businesses. With these successes in the private sector, the government privatized some business and began to actively encourage the creation of additional businesses.

While entrepreneurs and businesspeople are still encouraged to begin new businesses and operate as part of the free market economy, towns and villages are encouraged to begin and engage in various industries. These provide jobs for the people and improve incomes in the region. Called Township and Village Enterprises or TVE, these incorporate some traditional revolutionary values into the modern business world.

China has also encouraged foreign investment by creating special enterprise zones. These zones offer foreign companies significant incentives to build and operate factories in China, including reduced costs for land and lower taxes. These zones are designed near population centers, thereby providing a substantial source of inexpensive labor for the foreign factories.

Today, China is a significant world economic power, leading the world in manufacturing. Goods of all sorts are made in China and exported to the remainder of the world, both by Chinese-owned companies and foreign-owned companies operating out of China. This has reduced the cost of many consumer goods; however, quality issues are commonplace given the cheap manufacture and desire for cost-cutting.

3. **Describe the Iranian revolution of 1979, including at least three specific ways in which religion shaped this revolution.**

   Unlike other revolutions, including the Russian Revolution and Chinese Revolution, the Iranian Revolution was driven by religion. Other revolutions have traditionally been focused on social cleavages, including ethnicity or class, and economic conditions. The Iranian Revolution dramatically changed both the culture and politics of Iran, shaped specifically by a belief in not only Islam, but a specific Islamic leader, the Ayatollah Khomeini.

   The leader of the Iranian Revolution, the Ayatollah Khomeini, as Supreme Leader, held special status. While the state was organized as a theocracy, the Ayatollah was the clear and unquestioned leader of that theocracy and the final voice on matters of religion. He was a radical cleric, banned from the country for his past activities and encouragement of active revolution. During the revolution, after the overthrow of the Persian monarch, Ayatollah Khomeini was invited back into Iran to take his seat at the head of the government.

   The Iranian revolution occurred rapidly and in a nation experiencing significant prosperity, making it unusual. It had strong support from many elements in the public, largely on the basis of religious faith. Under the Shah, Iran had become increasingly secular, westernized and modern, all elements objected to by fundamentalist Muslims. The 1979 Revolution offered an alternative to those elements, blatantly rejecting them in favor of stringent religious law and policy.

   Under the new regime, the Iranian government was designed specifically to accommodate religious law, belief and expectation. While the government is, in name, democratic, the clerics hold the most substantial power. Individuals must be approved to run by the clerical Guardian Council and any action or press contrary to the laws of Islam is banned. This is the first government organized specifically around religious principles, to meet the demands of fundamentalist religious leaders.

   The 1979 Revolution was successful because of broad public support, even if the consequences of the revolution resulted in significant economic losses for the country. Today, Iran continues to struggle with the ramifications of those economic losses and while economic changes have been made, the faith-based theocratic government remains quite strong and legitimate.

Made in the USA
Middletown, DE
23 October 2021

50872931R00084